W9-ASH-685

Elegance in Flowers

Classic Arrangements for All Seasons

Written by Vicki L. Ingham

Paintings by Arthur Stewart
Photography by Sylvia Martin

Introduction by John Alex Floyd, Jr.

With Members of the
Women's Auxiliary of the
Birmingham Botanical Society

Virginia B. Bissell

Lula Rose T. Blackwell

Louise G. Smith

Carolyn D. Tynes

Arline F. Walter

Oxmoor
House®

Copyright 1985 by Oxmoor House, Inc.
Book Division of Southern Progress Corporation
P.O. Box 2463, Birmingham, Alabama 35201

All rights reserved. No part of this book may be reproduced in
any form or by any means without the prior written permission
of the Publisher, excepting brief quotations in connection with
reviews written specifically for inclusion in a magazine or
newspaper.

Library of Congress Catalog Number: 84-063031
ISBN: 0-8487-0642-0
Manufactured in the United States of America

Executive Editor: Candace Conard Bromberg
Production Manager: Jerry Higdon
Art Director: Bob Nance

First Edition

Elegance in Flowers

Editor: Cecilia C. Robinson
Editorial Assistants: Lisa Gant, Pamela Hall, Lenda Wyatt
Designer: Robin McDonald
Production Assistants: Rick Litton, Jane Bonds

FRONTISPIECE: *Spring Flowers with Apples,* watercolor, 30″ x 40″

Preface

When I moved to Birmingham almost ten years ago, I was immediately taken with the beauty of the region's flora. The one plant that really says "Birmingham" to me is the native oakleaf hydrangea, which seems to grow on almost every hillside in the city. As my circle of friends grew and I became more familiar with the horticultural and design community, I realized that just as oakleaf hydrangea was a Birmingham trademark, so were the massive line arrangements of flowers that I saw so often. It seemed that one of two statements was always made about the arrangements—that they were done by Lula Rose Blackwell or that they were done by a student of Beth McReynolds. In the last ten years, the refinement I have witnessed has been extraordinary. All the contributors to this book should be extremely proud of their design accomplishments. Their names are found on page 145.

Complementing their superior work is that of the design review team. For the last three years, these people have worked on evaluating the arrangements and making the selections for the book, which are truly outstanding. The review team members are not only great friends but also are among the great horticulturists and arrangers that grace this fine city.

In addition, I must thank Senior Garden Photographer Van Chaplin of Southern Living® for photographic help; Marc B. Reynolds of the Netherlands Flower-Bulb Institute for reviewing the portfolio of flowers; James Thomason, who helped so much in gathering materials and doing the mechanics for many of the arrangements; and the Women's Auxiliary of the Birmingham Botanical Society, of which most of the contributors are members. The publication of this book fulfills a long-held dream of many Auxiliary members.

For graciously allowing us to photograph in their homes, I would also like to thank Mr. and Mrs. Clarence B. Blair; Mr. and Mrs. Dixon Brooke, Jr.; Dr. and Mrs. David M. Comfort; Mr. and Mrs. Felix M. Drennen; Mr. and Mrs. George T. Gambrill III; Mr. and Mrs. John M. Harbert III; Mr. and Mrs. Wyatt R. Haskell; Mr. and Mrs. Carlisle Jones; Mr. and Mrs. T. Marcus McClellan, Jr.; Mr. and Mrs. William McTyeire; Mr. W. M. Miller; Mr. and Mrs. J. Reese Murray; Mr. and Mrs. Drayton Nabers, Jr.; Mrs. Alfred M. Shook III; Mr. and Mrs. Robert P. Shook; Miss Susan M. Shook; Mr. and Mrs. Elton B. Stephens, Jr.; Mr. Arthur Stewart; Mrs. Lee F. Turlington; Dr. and Mrs. Donald B. Williams; and Mr. and Mrs. John N. Wrinkle.

Some of the beautiful photographic locations were provided by the Country Club of Birmingham; Mountain Brook Club, Birmingham; Piedmont Driving Club, Atlanta; All Saints' Episcopal Church, Linville, North Carolina; Independent Presbyterian Church, Birmingham; St. Mary's Episcopal Church, Birmingham; and South Highland Presbyterian Church, Birmingham.

Vicki, Sylvia, and I hope that the beauty of the arrangements will inspire you to make fresh flowers a must for your home every day of the year.

John Alex Floyd, Jr.
Editor, SOUTHERN LIVING CLASSICS™

Introduction

When it comes to arranging flowers, style is the key word. Designs in many cases have been creative expressions on every imaginable theme, from period arrangements to avant-garde compositions. For many Southerners, however, elaborating on a particular theme is less important than making sure the treatment possesses elegance and a sense of fitness. This is especially true for the group of designers who composed the arrangements in this book. Flowers, foliage, and other objects used in the arrangements must be handled realistically, in a manner that is true to the nature of the materials as living, growing things. It would not be too extravagant a claim to say that the style featured in this book fits no exact category other than what many have characterized as the "Birmingham style."

The evolution of the style may be traced to a friendship. Beth McReynolds, who worked for a local florist, was trained in Japanese flower art and helped found Jefferson County Chapter 137 of Ikebana International. Lula Rose Blackwell was a young bride who enjoyed working with flowers. She became friends with Mrs. McReynolds and took lessons from her to learn the techniques of the florist's trade. When Mrs. Blackwell discovered the books of the legendary English flower designer Constance Spry, she shared them with Mrs. McReynolds, and the two learned the Spry approach together, stretching and changing it with the Japanese feeling for line and the distinctive quality of the local landscape materials and native Southern plants.

As arrangements in this exuberant style began appearing at weddings and parties, other people became interested in learning the new approach as well. To meet the demand, Mrs. McReynolds held classes in homes, teaching small groups of students to make arrangements using their own containers and flowers. The classes were immensely popular and helped to spread this approach to flower design throughout the city.

While there are no strict rules in this art, the principles are the same as in any art form. Designers also learn to look at materials in terms of their qualities of line, form, and color rather than their stereotyped category as florist's flower, garden blossom, wildflower, or "weed."

The motivating force is to make the realism of line and individual flower expression weave its way through the arrangement, whether this consists of a single flower or a massive bouquet. The grand displays are in fact particularly distinctive because the element of line is so predominant, and their complexity reveals the arranger's knowledge of design principles.

Blue Iris with Mixed Bouquet, *watercolor, 30" × 40"*

Calla Lilies and Dainty Bess Roses, *watercolor, 30" × 40"*

The importance of line and the manipulation of the elements of art give these arrangements traditional values with a fresh, modern, almost universal appeal. They can be as mixed as an English flower border but as simple as the first bloom of spring.

The selection of paintings by Arthur Stewart presented on these pages provides an opportunity to study the unique use of line and color blending as well as the diversity of approaches included in the Birmingham style. Arthur has been a great follower of this group of flower arrangers and has painted their work for many years. His paintings graphically demonstrate the English and Oriental influences found in this style and record years of design evolution and refinement.

One of the virtues of the style is its versatility. Arrangements may assume either formal or informal qualities. It should be noted, however, that the expression of formality is not in the exact repetition of material on either side of an imaginary line but rather in the choice of flowers and in the appropriateness of the design for its location: The arrangement takes on the formal essence of its setting. The same sense of place may be expressed with an informal arrangement in a casual setting. Thus, it is not the arrangements alone that are the hallmark of this book but the combination of the compositions and their suitability for the settings for which they are designed. As they become more and more accepted as a true floral style, they become not

Japanese Arrangement with Red Tulips, *watercolor, 40" × 50"*

Spring Arrangement with Blue Plate, *watercolor, 32" × 40"*

merely occasional decorative elements in an interior but an essential part of it.

The materials harvested for the flower arrangement are another key to the distinctive personalities of these designs. The foliage and branches that give the line are especially important. Elaeagnus is used so often that it is almost a byword among the designers, but a rich variety of other landscape materials is used as well. The reliance on the garden for many of the flowers and foliage used means that arrangements almost inevitably reflect the season. Spring and summer offer an abundance of flowers, grasses, and greenery. Autumn provides a palette of vivid hues with frost-touched leaves and late-blooming annuals and perennials. In winter, when flowers are scarce, fruit and evergreen foliage may be used instead to perform the same function. This is especially true at Christmas when swags and boughs mix greenery, berries, and fruit for a delightful fragrance and a colorful seasonal touch.

Twigs and branches with unusual character, berries and briars collected along roadsides, and all manner of exciting foliages can give designs a special touch. The results look natural, but finding just the right object is

Jonquils, Apples, and Lemons, *watercolor, 30" × 40"*

Spring Flowers with Camellias, *watercolor, 30" × 40"*

a labor of love. These materials, even more than the types of flowers, personalize the arrangements and make them special.

The book is divided into three major parts. Following the introduction is a section on arrangements for any occasion, which is subdivided into three smaller units: designs in which flowers dominate the arrangement, those in which flowers and foliages blend, and those in which foliage becomes not only the background but also the focus of visual interest.

The second major section of the book presents arrangements for special occasions, which include party, wedding, Christmas, and church flowers. As with flowers for everyday pleasure, compositions for such celebrations must fit the character of the setting. Most of the ones we show are somewhat grand—a special occasion certainly does not call for understated flowers. The mood expressed is always elegant and festive.

The final section is a portfolio of flowers, featuring Arthur Stewart's portraits of some of the flowers that are most frequently used in the arrangements. The portfolio also provides information on how to cut and

condition flowers to assure the longest possible vase life. The information here is based largely on the experience and expertise of Louise Smith, one of Birmingham's most respected horticulturists and gardeners.

While this is not a how-to book, the text attempts to give a sense of the construction of each arrangement, identifying its components and how they are used. The general procedure is often identical, but the same material can serve different functions in each arrangement. A flower that provides the focus for one arrangement, for example, may define the outline in another, according to the situation and the discretion of the individual designer.

The art of arranging flowers yields no permanent monument to the designer's skill. Its beauty is fleeting and for that reason is all the more poignant. Elegance in Flowers attempts to document the creativity of the flower arrangers in Birmingham and to celebrate the expression of what is indeed an artistic gift.

Dutch Arrangement, *watercolor, 22" × 30"*

Arrangements for All Seasons

Elegance in Flowers

A mound of summer flowers embellished with fruit creates a lush centerpiece for the dining table. Building the arrangement requires both a wealth of flowers and reserves of patience and skill, because it must be designed to present a pleasing face to each side. At the same time, the whole group must be knit together without seams.

Snapdragons and large, spiny cactus dahlias establish the framework. Using an odd number of stems keeps the arrangement from developing a blocky, square shape. The stems stretch toward each end of the table and to each side, wedged into the florist's foam at slight angles to prevent stiffness. The top stems are also placed off-center to assure a loose, rounded crown. Alstroemeria and additional cactus dahlias fill out the main lines.

Focal points are then established so that on each side there will be a place for the eye to rest. An exquisite pink garden rose dominates the view that will greet guests as they enter the dining room. It is placed high in the design, where its luminous quality and clear color set the tone of elegance for the group.

Shaping the dome of rich color then proceeds with garden-grown dahlias, roses, and zinnias in shades of red, pink, red orange, and magenta. Pale pink florist's chrysanthemums add highlights. Lavender ageratum, purple lantana, and deep purple lisianthus (an imported flower) provide jewel-like accents that enhance the rose pink theme. The colors are worked in one at a time to ensure a balanced distribution through the arrangement. Care is also taken to provide variety in scale by mingling small, medium, and large face flowers and punctuating them with tightly closed buds. Flowers are allowed to extend below the edge of the silver compote that holds the florist's foam. This softens the baseline for a more pleasing effect.

Panicles of bright green peegee hydrangea are worked in next to complement the pink flowers and provide contrasting form and texture. Small heads are pushed in deep to serve as foils for the cactus dahlias. Other stems reach down toward the table and stretch up to the chandelier, enriching the shape.

For the finishing touch, plump grapes, lemons, grapefruit, and pomegranates are arranged to embrace the compote. To link more closely the flowers and fruit, pink cactus dahlias are inserted into florist's water vials and tucked among the fruit, and bright yellow marigolds are added to the arrangement to balance the citrus.

Roses are considered aristocrats among flowers. Queen Anne's lace, although often overlooked as a lowly roadside weed, also offers an effect that is as regal as its name. When the two are joined with single-flowered dahlias, the result is a delightful partnership. Arranged against the muted blue gray tones of a watercolor, the pure yellow roses are sunny but not overwhelming. The quiet background plays up the delicate lines and airy feeling of the arrangement.

The shape that is developed in the footed brass bowl is a simple triangular one. To keep it from becoming static and rigid, flowers and foliage break the edge of the vase and fall casually below it. In addition, each flower is positioned so that none faces the viewer directly. This gives the arrangement a relaxed, natural look and suggests movement through the composition.

Dahlias define the outline of the triangle. The open blooms recall fresh-faced daisies, while the buds offer distinctive personality to the arrangement's silhouette.

Queen Anne's lace is added next to stretch the outline higher and wider and bring the design forward. Garden roses fill out the framework. The full-blown blossoms may have a shorter vase life than would partly opened buds, but they have a softer, looser quality and give more color value. A few rosebuds are also used to repeat the form of the unopened dahlias and to add dimension to the design. Blue sage (salvia) supplies accent and depth.

To complete the arrangement, begonia, dahlia, and rose leaves are tucked in at the base and among the roses. The foliage helps hide the mesh-covered florist's foam and serves as an undershadow that sets off the flowers. For a finishing touch that gives the flowers added importance and impact, the arrangement is lifted on a simple black stand with scrolled ends.

When flowers in the entry are presented on a tall pedestal stand, they gain importance as an expression of welcome. Here the felicitous combination of dogwood and forsythia radiates a blithe and cheerful spirit, bringing a sense of the season indoors.

Dogwood branches provide both outline and lacy mass, defining a triangle whose arms flow well below the base of the arrangement. The branches, pruned from trees in the landscape, are selected carefully to avoid damaging the shapes of the trees. The posture of each branch guides its best use, and the dogwood's natural manner of holding the flowers aloft on upturned branches gives the flower faces a sense of presentation. To inject a feeling of movement into the composition, branches are inserted with a slight twist so that all the flowers do not face directly forward.

Forsythia branches embellish the framework, superimposing a relaxed S-curve over the triangle and bringing the design forward. Flexing the branches before inserting them in the arrangement gives them a more graceful line. Additional branches carry the color through for balance.

Bunches of yellow chrysanthemums are then worked in to strengthen the impact of yellow. Orange lilies and tulips are added last, giving intensity and depth to the color scheme. Tucking the deepest oranges among the branches helps draw the eye into and through the design. The petals of the tulips are gently forced open to gain an even greater value of color from the enormous, chalicelike blooms.

To finish, stems of winter honeysuckle are added, reinforcing the outline while preserving the airy quality derived from the open, linear character of the dogwood. Arum lilies hide the underpinnings of florist's foam covered with wire mesh. The cascading effect of this arrangement renders the container insignificant so that the emphasis is on the composition and its role as a piece of art.

When flowers will be seen from above (*previous page*), the meticulous designer is careful to ensure that the arrangement is as pleasing from the foreshortened view as it is when seen from the more usual angles. This mass of spring flowers, placed near a stairway, presents a pleasing aspect to guests looking down into the arrangement as they ascend or descend the stairs. It is also designed to be enjoyed by those in the foyer below, where the console table stands.

The palette is restricted to blues, pinks, and tones of red, which take on dramatic brilliance against the black table and mirror frame. Imported anemones supply the bulk of the color spectrum, supplemented by Dutch irises, pink chrysanthemums and azaleas, and a bit of red violet liatris.

The arrangement is composed by working with one color at a time, beginning with the medium tones and moving to the darker and lighter colors respectively. The initial flowers indicate the height, width, and focus, and the remaining flowers are then positioned with reference to these. The French brass bowl calls for a formal shape, so the focal area is placed at the center front. A pair of red anemones extending from the base directs attention into this area and beyond it to the crown of the group, which is marked by anemones and a chrysanthemum.

To create movement through the composition, flowers are then placed to suggest paths of color that cross through the design diagonally from front to back. Flowers that look to the side or the rear reinforce this sense of movement, but most of the blossoms are positioned to face upward, giving the full value of their color to the bird's-eye perspective. To keep the composition from seeming too dense, it is enriched with a feeling of depth by recessing some of the flowers quite deeply into the group and allowing others to project above them. At the rim of the container the recessed flowers give a gentler line to the base of the design.

To finish, Lenten roses are tucked in on each side to elongate the arrangement and to provide refreshing contrast to the bright colors. Mock orange flowers with the foliage intact serve as filler to hide the underpinnings of florist's foam. The white blossoms also help highlight and separate the flowers so that their colors can be read more clearly. Heath is inserted last, providing a wispy, graceful line that relaxes the arrangement. Stems reach into the mirror, beyond the table's edge, and forward from the body of the group to give it a lighter, airier quality.

The practice of using landscape materials to give a seasonal accent to an arrangement communicates a sense of continuity between garden and interiors. Redbud, flowering cherry, and spring bulbs define the character of this group. Purchased flowers supply color and form to enhance these garden materials.

The flowering branches and two types of commercially grown greenery (myrtle and ruscus) go in first to establish a fan shape. This shape offers the right note of formality for the container, a gilded urn. To prevent stiffness, the upright branches are angled slightly toward the wall, and the lowest ones are positioned to arch beyond the edge of the table.

The heavy-stemmed materials—snapdragons, delphiniums, heather, and tulips—are inserted next, further defining the shape toward which the designer works. Delphiniums and tulips also bring the line forward from the heart of the group. Because the focal area is being saved for camellias, the red tulips are used as intermediate flowers so that they accent and enliven the group without dominating it.

The arrangement is then filled in with freesias, Lenten roses, and a variety of daffodils. Because daffodil stems are not sturdy, a hole is first made in the florist's foam with a wooden pick. Then the stem can be inserted.

The camellias are worked in as the composition progresses. The fragile flowers are tucked in deep to soften the edge of the urn and to anchor the stems and branches that stretch and spread from the focal area. Daffodils and a stem of delphinium are pulled forward to float above them, creating depth.

The composition is finished with candytuft, bits of heather, and two kinds of chrysanthemums worked in to fill gaps and provide transition between the outermost blossoms and those at the center. The palette in this group ranges from blue violet and lavender to red violet, red, pink, white, and vivid yellow. Flowers are positioned with an eye to the pleasing harmony with or contrast to adjacent hues. The framework of heather and redbud and the even distribution of yellow through the fan shape help to ensure an impression of unity and balance.

The graceful shape of this exuberant bouquet is made possible by a foundation of florist's foam which overfills the urn. Wire mesh is taped over the foam to help hold it together under the weight of so many stems and branches.

A few special flowers from the spring garden can set the mood for the whole arrangement. Here giant double peonies offer a lush romantic look that is enhanced by the lacy effect of mock orange and mountain laurel.

When the flowers are arranged in concert with the oval mirror, the composition expresses a delicate, lyrical quality that is as delightful and evanescent as the season itself.

Branches of Japanese maple and mock orange go in first to describe a crescent shape cradling the mirror. Twigs and leaves are scissored off the mock orange branches to accent their searching line and dainty white flowers. One maple branch is also trimmed slightly for a lighter effect and inserted in profile, reaching to the tabletop. To balance the strong thrust of the crescent, additional maple and mock orange are secured on the opposite side, arching beyond the edge of the table. In order to achieve the desired line, the mock orange is inserted to show the underside of the flowers and leaves. Viewed this way, the flowers recall dogwood blossoms.

Bearded irises reinforce the outline, and an orange tulip stretches the crescent still further. A yellow-and-red tulip balances it to form a long, graceful arc sweeping up through the group of flowers.

This framework is then filled in one color at a time to ensure a balanced composition. Yellow Dutch irises, snapdragons, and alstroemeria are clustered for greater impact on either side of the center. This is left free for the most important flower, the huge pink peony. Next, clusters of mountain laurel are positioned to fall softly over the edge of the vase. Between the two, carmine roses are recessed into the arrangement. Their intense, flawless color gives weight to the focus, throwing the lighter tints into sharp relief.

Red violet peonies balance the roses and lift the eye upward. Additional pink roses and pink and white peonies fill out the body of the arrangement, carrying the eye around it to the mirror. To make the reflection as rich and full as the front of the composition, blossoms are worked in close at the back. To finish, lavender and purple delphiniums and Dutch irises are added to intensify the reds, rusts, and yellows.

One element in the appeal of this composition is the way it is worked in combination with the mirror, creating the illusion of lavish depth. To raise the arrangement high enough so this conjury is possible, the container is placed on a simple Ming-type stand. Florist's foam projects several inches above the rim of the iron bowl holding the flowers. This permits the insertion of stems at low angles to create the fluid line that gives the design its grace.

In focusing attention on the painting above the mantel, this simple arrangement increases its own impact as well.

The flattering effect is achieved by breaking into the picture with branches and flowers so that they suggest a foreground framing the vista beyond.

Leafless branches of hawthorn define the dynamic, asymmetric framework. Armed with twiggy spurs and ornamented with red berries, the branches have a halting, gestural quality that gives the design an expressive character. The longest branch is inserted first to cut boldly across the picture plane. An upturned branch balances it, cradling the painting. Additional hawthorn then fills in this shape and carries the line below the mantel for a loose, graceful effect.

Stems of euphorbia and freesia go in next to reinforce the skeleton of branches. Removing their foliage enhances the linear quality as well as the note of yellow they add. However, color is subordinated to line where necessary, and two tall stems of euphorbia are placed to face the painting in order to obtain the desired upward sweep.

Garden roses and dahlias in tints and shades of peach, orange, and pink are then worked in. Allowing the dahlias to extend below the mantel gives the group a natural, casual grace. Two kinds of yellow dahlias are positioned next. Reaching into the picture plane and plunging below the mantel, the flowers set up a dynamic tension with the strength of their line and color.

Fuji and Red Rover chrysanthemums and yellow statice help tie the design together. For depth, a single Fuji chrysanthemum is tucked at the back of the arrangement, and yellow statice is recessed at the focal point. For the finishing touch, yellow pincushion chrysanthemums are added as filler. Care is taken not to overfill the vase, however. Leaving voids in the design gives the individual flowers definition and permits them to show to best advantage.

To achieve lines that project well below the base of the arrangement, the stems must be inserted at low angles. For this arrangement, the low metal container is filled with florist's foam that projects above the rim by an amount equal to the height of the container.

howy garden flowers massed on the mantel recall the arrangements that were rendered with precision in seventeenth-century Dutch flower paintings. The portrait above the mantel serves the same purpose as the umber backgrounds used in those paintings, highlighting the perfection and brilliance of the individual flowers. Unlike the groupings in such art, however, all of these flowers bloom during the same season and were gathered from an early summer garden.

Oakleaf hydrangea establishes the width and lowest point of the design. The branches were stripped of leaves to heighten the impact of the great cone-shaped flower clusters. Three stems of hosta flowers (plantain lily), with most of the bell-like blooms still in bud, form a curving spray that carries the eye from the top of the design through the focal point to a panicle of oakleaf hydrangea extending below the mantel. With this framework in place, hosta foliage is inserted to conceal the container—a simple, low rectangular vase.

Building the design then proceeds with pink roses, which follow the lines and movement begun by the oakleaf hydrangea. Although the base of the arrangement is clearly established at the mantel edge, that edge is broken by the flowers falling below it, giving the group a graceful quality.

Panicles of blue hydrangea are placed next to lead the eye in and out of the design as well as across it. At the focal area, two large garden lilies, a cluster of coral roses, and orange gerbera daisies are massed for bright color. Orange and pale yellow daylilies, creamy garden lilies, yarrow, roses, and gerbera daisies then fill out the design, and a lavender garden lily strengthens the impact of the hosta flowers at the top. Daylilies must be replaced daily, but their bright colors and starry flower forms have a summertime appeal that is difficult to resist bringing indoors.

Although designers generally advise against dotting flowers singly through an arrangement, solitary stems of black-eyed Susans are used effectively here for contrasting flower size and shape. They also provide a bright accent. Balloon flowers are tucked in behind one yellow garden lily and close to the crown of the design. Their rich deep tone intensifies the color values of the other flowers and adds the extra spark that brings the group to life.

In an arrangement of closely packed flowers such as this, the only need for foliage is at the base to hide the container and mesh-covered florist's foam. A few leaves were left on the roses and the hydrangea close to the flower heads, however, to help draw water up to the blossoms.

When potted flowers are the starting point for an arrangement, the result is a lively microcosm of the garden. The composition fairly bursts with the natural vitality of growing things.

The size of the basket determines the number of plants that can be accommodated. This one is wide enough to hold an interesting variety, but it is also quite deep. To bring the pots level with the rim of the basket, it is first lined with a brown plastic bag and filled with blocks of water-soaked florist's foam. Then, because the arrangement is intended to be seen primarily from the front and sides, pots of lilies are placed toward the rear and pots of gerbera daisies toward the front, where leaves and one flower soften the basket's edge. Tulips go in to provide transition. Kalanchoe and *Exacum* are worked in on the far side of the handle, which is allowed to show in order to retain the feeling of a garden basket. The *Exacum*, a good low-light plant, spills over the edge to broaden the group and add lush texture.

To complete the arrangement, cut anemones and candytuft are inserted into the florist's foam on which the pots rest. The candytuft fills in at the center, creating a low path of white that sweeps around the tulips and links the kalanchoe with the flowers in the foreground. Pushing the candytuft in deep also gives variation in the layers of color and texture, adding interest to the composition. Anemones provide a balance of color and pick up the note of red in the potted bromeliad that is inserted at the back for interest. For the finishing touch, Spanish moss is tucked in all around to cover the underpinnings and the pots.

The arrangement will stay fresh for days if the pots are kept watered and the florist's foam remoistened (hence the need for a plastic liner in the basket).

When the subject of a painting is related to flowers or gardening, an arrangement can add a startling third dimension, enhancing the artwork in an exciting and satisfying way. Gilbert Gaul's painting *Lady and the Hollyhocks* inspired this arrangement of spring flowers in a basket. The flowers, keyed to the colors in the canvas, are composed in an informal manner for a fresh, spontaneous look.

Queen Anne's lace and snapdragons establish the highest point and the width. Allowing stems to project across the picture frame emphasizes the relationship between the arrangement and the art. Flowers reaching from the edge of the basket and beyond the table give a loose, natural quality to the shape. The snapdragons also add a lively touch with strongly curling tips, which help lead the eye around the design. Pink tulips further define the shape, carrying color to the edges of the group. Instead of placing all of the flowers to radiate from the center of the basket, some are positioned to face each other, giving the arrangement a sense of growth and life. Miniature pink carnations are added to carry the pink theme through the design. As the flowers are worked in, care is taken to let the handle and bottom of the basket show.

With the overall shape defined, hosta leaves and Lenten roses are inserted to cover the underpinnings. Hosta also curls over the edge of the basket to reinforce the snapdragons that bring the design forward.

Red, lavender, and blue anemones and two stems of violet camassia are then worked in, filling out the shape and giving depth to the color spectrum. There are only two stems of camassia, which is an imported bulb, so they are placed toward the front to take advantage of their height, color, and unusual form.

Red gerbera daisies balance the red anemones. One gerbera daisy goes in quite low at the front for a vivid note that gives the arrangement focus. Another toward the rear helps draw the eye around the basket.

Narcissus and bridal wreath spirea finish the arrangement along with a few last stems of Queen Anne's lace, which provide a soft, fine texture that sets off the tulips.

To provide the underpinnings, a plastic liner fits into the basket and is filled with florist's foam. Wire mesh is taped over the top of the foam for security.

he impact that an arrangement makes is often a matter of proportion. An exuberant display that dominates the setting declares the occasion special. Here the flowers are composed to take advantage of the picture on the wall beyond so that it frames them. This links them to the setting and at the same time emphasizes their central importance in the dining room.

Snapdragons define the height and width, forming a fan-shaped outline and bringing the line forward. To prevent the impression of ''horns,'' the intermediate stems are inserted at different depths.

Yellow tulips embellish the framework. To give the greatest possible impact, their petals are gently forced back so that the flowers form broad parasols of color. Pink lilies are then worked in to describe a broad curve through the group. The lowest lily breaks the edge of the bowl, bringing color low in the design. The lily at the heart of the arrangement is tucked in deep so that its budded stem projects forward in front of it. This creates a sense of depth while disrupting the impact of the flower's color, giving the line of lilies more subtlety. An additional stalk of lilies, placed to balance the top one, is positioned to face toward the rear, further enhancing the sense of depth.

Delphiniums and dill are then worked in. The blue violet of the delphiniums snaps the other colors to life, while their spiky forms reinforce that of the snapdragons. Dill provides soft fullness and adds an unexpected touch that gives interest to the group.

Grasses and corkscrew willow are inserted next, wedged in among the flowers. These materials offer a fluid, unrestrained quality that loosens the shape and adds personality to the composition.

Finally, Spanish moss is tucked in all around the underpinnings to hide the florist's foam. Raising the glass bowl on a carved stand enhances the arrangement's airy quality, and placing it on a mirror is the final elegant flourish.

he lavish display of most spring-blooming trees is fleeting. Bringing a few boughs indoors provides an opportunity to enjoy the soft colors and delicate textures at closer range. These thickly flowered branches of a hybrid crabapple offer an airy, elegant quality that lends itself well to formal compositions.

The branches are inserted to define a graceful fan. To ensure a relaxed shape, three branches are used to mark the apex, and the longest limb breaks the edge of the console table. Because the boughs are so densely covered with flowers, short pieces are pruned from the bottom portion. This cleans up the branch and allows it to slip more easily into the foundation. The bits that are trimmed off fill in around the base of the group.

Orange lilies, yellow lilies, and freesias are then worked in. The tulips offer the strongest contrast to the form of the crabapple, so they are given primary importance in the group. The flowers bring the color of the background into the composition, carrying it high into the arrangement and reaching toward the console table to reinforce the branches. To make sure their impact is felt, the tulips in the body of the group are placed in front of the crabapple. Some of the stems

need assistance to gain the necessary height. Inserting them in florist's water vials, which are then wired to hyacinth sticks, helps achieve the desired placement.

The lilies and freesias highlight the shape and fill voids in the outline. Kaffir lilies are then added to reinforce the tulips and carry the line well below the base of the arrangement.

To finish, several types of narcissus are worked in through the group, forming overlapping triangles that provide depth and fullness. The faces are turned to look at each other to give the composition personality. The hollow stems can be difficult to insert in florist's foam, but carefully pushing a length of florist's wire into the stem makes them easier to work into the foundation. Leatherleaf fern is then used to hide the underpinnings and provide undershadow.

For this composition, the container is as important to the overall effect as the flowers and their placement. Like the crabapple that sets the mood, the silver coffee urn is formal and graceful, with sleek lines that enhance the airy quality of the group. To receive the stems, it is overfilled with florist's foam which is covered with wire mesh. The lid serves to strengthen the link between the flowers and console table. The shattered blossoms beside it are a final flourish that softens the formality with an artless, natural touch.

resh flowers call attention to important objects in a natural and personal way. Choosing flowers with colors that relate to the setting ensures that the arrangement will fit into the whole scheme of decoration as naturally as the objects they enhance. This arrangement in yellow and green ties together two pieces, the Romanoff crystal urn and the portrait above, to create a single elegant composition.

Wild hawthorn establishes the shape and projects across the canvas to frame the figure. The branches are pruned lightly to accent their linear quality and keep them from seeming too heavy for the urn. In addition, turning one of the top branches in profile gives a more interesting effect.

Viburnum is worked in next. Most of the flower buds are still tightly closed, giving the heads a light green tint. The larger flower heads are placed to reinforce the shape, and smaller bits are tucked in the interior to carry the color through.

Tulips are then placed to describe a broad arc. One blossom is also tucked in at the rim of the urn to carry the eye into the group. Yellow lilies are clustered above this tulip to supply focus. Additional stalks are placed higher in the group to lift the eye and are tucked deep into the back to provide fullness. The hint of color that can be glimpsed among the other stems also gives depth.

Narcissus, freesias, Lenten roses, and bits of pearlbush finish the design. Inserted for a balanced distribution of color, the flowers provide the variety in scale that makes for a better design. Blossoms also go in low to soften the rim of the container and bring the design below it. A few stems tucked at the rear keep the arrangement from looking flat if it is seen from the side.

To underscore the beauty of the crystal vase, the stems are not allowed to project into it. Instead, they are kept short and are carefully inserted into a foundation of crumpled wire mesh that is fixed into the top of the urn. Such a foundation requires patience in working with the natural weight of the stems, which affects how they tend to rest in the container.

lowers displayed above eye level serve to draw the gaze upward, providing a sense of lift. A high chest offers a good height, raising the flowers enough for impact but not so high that graceful vertical lines cannot be developed.

Short branches of leucothoe sketch in the main lines, indicating an asymmetrical shape that fills the corner and reaches toward the center of the chest. Forsythia elaborates on this framework, stretching toward the ceiling, out to the side, and forward. Although the posture of each stem suggests its best use, the oddly jointed growth of one branch is used to special advantage, carrying the eye out to the edge and back into the heart of the arrangement. White camellias are then inserted. The large, soft faces form a low mound, giving each of the two views a place for the eye to rest.

With the outline and focus in place, completing the arrangement is a matter of filling in with intermediate flowers that link the two. Ranunculuses strengthen the yellow-and-white theme. To underscore the feeling of movement, the flowers are placed to radiate from the focal area.

Daffodils also reinforce the impression of energy and depth. Each flower is angled differently, so that some present profiles while others offer a three-quarter view or face directly forward. Blossoms also reach below the edge of the container, giving a more graceful line to the base of the arrangement. Finally, freesias are placed to balance the camellias by carrying the note of white to the outer edges of the arrangement.

To provide a sufficiently ample container for the display, a tureen on a platter is pressed into service and filled with florist's foam. Wire mesh covers the foam and is wired to the handles for security. The gilded lid of the tureen serves as the accessory that supplies the finishing touch.

17

The materials available from the garden at any given time provide much of the inspiration for an arrangement. Here Southern crabapple is the starting point for a combination of pink, lavender, and purple flowers arranged in an amethyst Venetian glass vase. The monochromatic scheme that results is cool and refined.

Crabapple is positioned in the foundation first to describe a fan. Branches are inserted at the rim of the vase to fall to the piano, giving a loose, graceful effect. To prevent stiffness at the apex, the tallest vertical branch is reinforced by a second shorter one. Additional branches then bring the line forward and trace broad, counterbalancing curves through the design. To stress the irregular, linear quality of the branches, leaves are selectively scissored off. This also plays up the value of the pastel flowers and dark pink buds.

Holland-grown tulips are then worked in. Satiny purple and pink lily-flowering ones embellish the framework, underscoring its fountainlike form with their long, arching stems. Placing the tallest tulips to look toward the rear adds depth and interest. A pair of purple tulips extends below the edge of the vase, balancing those at the crown and bringing the design forward. These tulips also help obscure the outline of the mechanics, which are barely discernible through the glass. Unusual red-and-white tulips are tucked in deep at the focus and added through the arrangement for highlight and contrast. All of the tulip stems are wrapped with florist's wire to ensure that their graceful lines will be maintained. Otherwise, the tulips will tend to wander toward the light.

Delphiniums are then worked in to enliven the color scheme. Their flower spikes have a delicate effect that enhances the light, ethereal quality that is needed for a glass vase.

Thick bunches of heather fill out the composition, strengthening it at the center and adding fullness at the sides and back.

The flowing contours that give the arrangement its grace require a foundation of florist's foam that projects well above the rim of the container. Foam sometimes leaves a sediment in the container, however. To prevent this, the florist's foam is placed in a plastic liner that rests in the mouth of the vase. For stability, the liner is secured to a wire that encircles the neck of the vase.

Flowers (*overleaf*) for a seated dinner can easily form a barrier between guests unless the arrangement is lifted above eye level. A three-light silver candelabrum accomplishes this nicely, raising the bouquet so that it has dramatic impact without obstructing conversation across the table.

To link the flowers to the setting, the designer took her cue from the tablecloth and draperies, choosing flowers of mauve, lavender, rosy pink, clear blue, and bright green. A tall spike of bells-of-Ireland serves as the axis for the arrangement; placing this spike at an angle gives the composition a slight twist that keeps it from being stiff or static.

Tulips and carnations go in next to define a fan shape; completing the group is then a matter of filling in this shape. Because it will be seen in the round, the flowers must radiate in all directions, with the faces looking toward the ceiling and the floor as well as to the guests. Each flower's virtues suggest its best use. The full, fluffy heads of carnations and chrysanthemums, for example, give a sense of solidity and a strong effect of color, so they are primarily concentrated in the center of the group. To intensify the effect of mauve, a few of the larger chrysanthemums are tucked in close at the base. The stiff stems of delphiniums and Dutch irises, on the other hand, offer a strong vertical note, so they are placed near the top to lift the eye upward.

To stress color and line, most of the foliage is removed from the flowers, except from the stems of waxflower; its feathery foliage and tiny red violet flowers add fullness. Drooping leucothoe, turned to show its bright green underside, is tucked in to hide the arrangement's underpinnings.

A design such as this one has some special requirements. It calls for a small bowl that fits into the candle cup. This is available from flower shops and holds florist's foam covered with wire mesh. To keep the foam and wire support from shifting, they should be secured to the container with florist's tape.

The slender proportions of the candelabrum further require that only small and medium-size flowers be used. Large ones would appear top-heavy, and those with big stems would take up too much of the florist's foam, making it difficult to insert as many stems as are needed to create a full bouquet.

Finally, the group should be composed with the candles in place so that the blossoms will be clear of the flames when the candles are lighted.

*L*ike music, flowers (*previous page*) speak a universal language. A brilliant display on the piano expresses the importance of the occasion, suggesting that every care has been taken to make the evening a memorable one.

For the container, a silver wine cooler is pressed into service. It sets a tone of formal elegance and lifts the flowers for a more graceful, fluid effect.

As befits an urn-type vase, the outline assumes a fan shape. The character of each branch governs its placement. Long pieces of elaeagnus and a bare privet branch establish the crown. Arching branches of yaupon holly and sasanqua camellias balance each other to form an S-curve that defines the width. This line flows through the design with a balletic grace, setting into motion a rhythmic energy that is expressed with additional sasanqua camellias and yaupon holly, privet berries, variegated Oregon holly, and Burford holly.

The rubrum and yellow lilies are positioned next. There are only two stems of each, and placing them early permits the designer to give them the necessary prominence. Rubrum lilies carry the color theme to the crown and draw the eye to the top of the composition. One stalk of yellow lilies is framed between branches of variegated Oregon holly, where the flowers bring out the color in the edges of the foliage. The yellow also gives definition to a portion of the arrangement that might otherwise be lost against the dark painting behind it. To gain depth, the second stalk of yellow lilies is placed to face the wall so that its hint of color lures the eye through the composition.

White lilacs go in next to balance the yellow lilies. The flowers introduce fragrance as well, adding another dimension to the pleasure imparted by the arrangement.

The composition is then built up by color, using carnations, tulips, roses, narcissus, euphorbia, and daisy chrysanthemums. The vivid reds are concentrated primarily around the middle of the group. Against the lavender walls, the effect is electrifying. Carnations and tulips are also inserted to fall below the rim of the vase, loosening and softening the shape.

White and pink flowers supply highlights and underline the sense of movement through the composition. At the heart of the design, a magenta carnation, metallic pink miniature carnations, and lavender freesias are clustered to suggest a "bosom" of color. This is reinforced by a large rose pink camellia, which softens the edge of the wine cooler and anchors the spray of flowers. A second camellia is placed toward the side where the pianist or a guest can enjoy it.

Orange euphorbia is then worked in. The broadly arching stems, stripped of foliage, accent the outline.

At the bosom, the bright orange hue snaps life into the red and pink scheme.

To finish, purple Dutch irises are worked in, adding a note of violet that intensifies the other colors. Miniature carnations and heather provide filler.

While a natural, graceful line is always desirable, tulips have a tendency to lean toward the strongest source of light. For a formal arrangement such as this one, therefore, the stems are wired to keep the color where it should stay. To obtain a stronger value of red from the tulips and carnations, the designer breathes lightly on the flower face and gently pushes the petals further open.

To form a tall foundation that helps stems gain the necessary height, florist's foam is stacked in the wine cooler. Wire mesh keeps the foam from breaking apart under the weight of the material.

A visual symphony results when flowers express the same graceful character as their setting. Here, the fine proportions of the Venetian mirror and the French demilune table call for light, delicate flowers.

Native Southern Piedmont azaleas answer with a gossamer quality and the same soft pink that tints the Venetian swan vase. This native azalea, sometimes called wild honeysuckle, has a sparse, linear growth. The branches hold the flower clusters aloft so that they seem suspended in air, giving a misty, ethereal effect. The repetition of the arrangement's shape in the framed antique fan and mirror subtly links these elements into a tightly composed whole.

Pruning the branches from shrubs in the garden requires a selective eye. The gardener must cut a sufficient number of shapely branches for a full bouquet without marring the shape of the shrubs or their display outdoors. For this design, the young, unfolding foliage is left on the branches. Its soft texture and color underscore the impact of the flowers.

The only flower support is the stems themselves. Developing the fan shape as a natural extension of the vase requires balancing the branches against each other. The contour and weight of each stem suggest its best placement, but branches are trimmed as necessary to give the desired fullness. The shrub's growth habit almost automatically assures a sense of depth and movement in the design.

Like the season, the delicate blooms of flowering shrubs are fleeting. However, they can last up to seven days if the branch ends are split about one inch and then placed in tepid water overnight.

lowers and artwork are natural companions, and the partnership is happiest when the colors of one complement and intensify those of the other. Against the emerald green sea in this canvas, the pink and red flowers snap to life, giving an effect that is crisp, clean, and rich.

Graceful branches of redbud establish strong diagonals that lead the eye across the painting, and secondary counterbalancing branches help frame the subject of the artwork. Snapdragons accent these lines. Camellias are then inserted in the place of honor, with the lowest blossoms placed at the bowl's rim for a richer effect.

Tulips are worked in next, positioned to take advantage of their gracefully twisted stems. Placing the pink ones high and toward the rear of the arrangement and the red ones low and forward subtly suggests the same atmospheric perspective used in the painting. This gives the arrangement a light, airy feeling and a sense of dimension.

A pair of yellow freesias is added next for a brilliant sunlit quality. Delphiniums and daisy chrysanthemums then go in to stretch the framework. Stems of the darker delphiniums are also added to the body of the group to provide a note of blue violet that enhances the other colors.

To finish, daffodils, candytuft, heather, and Lenten roses are worked in. Because there are only a few daffodils and they are light in color, the stems are paired for greater impact. Candytuft and Lenten roses spill over the edge of the bowl for a loose, casual effect. Care is taken, however, not to hide the bowl entirely, because it is a fine Oriental piece that brings together all of the flower colors.

A generous mound of florist's foam fills the bowl to receive the stems. A pad of wire mesh covers the foam. When tree branches such as the redbud are cut for bringing indoors, it is important that the gardener prune carefully. The need for branches with pleasing lines must be balanced with a concern for maintaining the shape of the tree.

An exuberant mass of spring flowers assumes an almost ethereal quality when it is elevated on a brass pedestal vase. This is especially striking when the flowers will be seen across a roomful of guests: Lifting the arrangement ensures that it will have the decorative impact needed for a festive occasion. To achieve the desired height, the vase is placed on a carved wooden stand. The stand also visually links the mass of flowers to the table, suggesting an anchor for the floating composition.

To begin, branches of Japanese maple rough in the outline. These main lines are accented and extended with branches of mock orange, defining a classic Hogarth curve. Additional mock orange inserted on each side forms a relaxed horizontal line that counterweights the vertical, suggesting the controlled balance of a dancer on pointe. Snipping off most of the foliage allows the porcelain white blossoms to show up brilliantly against the persimmon-colored walls. Removing the leaves also helps the flowers to last longer.

To give solidity to the center and base of the arrangement, branches of mountain laurel are tucked low in the design. With most of the buds still tightly closed, the flower clusters form a lacy swath of soft pink through the heart of the design.

Once the woody-stemmed material is in place, the flowers are worked in. Because only a few stems of each type are used, they are clustered by color to increase their impact. Lemon yellow snapdragons, alstroemeria, and butter-colored irises are loosely grouped on either side of the axis, accenting and counterbalancing the ascending curve. Two orange-and-red tulips carry strong color high into the design. A similar pair marks the focus, with the outer petals of one tulip gently forced open for a stronger color value. Purple Dutch irises, delphiniums, and lavender amsonia are inserted along the line of the principal curve to intensify the effect of the yellows and reds. Two camellias are then tucked in low to strengthen the effect of the mountain laurel. Inserting the stems in florist's water vials gives the needed height and provides water to prolong the life of the flowers.

For the finishing touch, a few leaves of variegated hosta (plantain lily) are pushed deep into the arrangement to hide the foundation, a large block of florist's foam covered with wire mesh.

Between the grand occasions, humbler bouquets give a simpler, more intimate pleasure. This small group freshens the coffee table with life and color. It is kept low to avoid interfering with conversation.

Garden greenery establishes the outline, which is three-dimensional so that the arrangement can be enjoyed from all sides. The crown is defined with two stems of Florida leucothoe and a flower stalk of hosta (plantain lily) stripped of its blossoms. Additional leucothoe and azalea and Japanese maple branches establish the base and carry the line toward the table.

Tangerine-striped carnations reinforce the crown. Pink and peach dahlias and a deep red chrysanthemum are inserted next, concentrated low in the design, where they soften the edge of the bowl and give the composition a focus. A single red dahlia brings a note of intense color to the top of the design for balance. Chrysanthemums, miniature carnations, and roses then fill out the body of the group. Their colors—pink, lavender, peach, and yellow—are drawn from the delicately tinted petals of the dahlias. To make sure each color can be read clearly, stems are clustered by twos and threes. Allowing some of the flowers to project from the body of the arrangement carves the space around it into voids, giving the composition a loose, airy feeling.

The arrangement is assembled quickly on a foundation of water-soaked florist's foam. Lifting the bowl on a carved stand is a simple but effective way to stress the group's light quality.

Framing a special painting with flowers calls attention to the artwork and gives the flowers more importance as well. Here colors drawn from the jars, Chinese pillow, and Della Dryer's study of a young woman provide the palette that finds brilliant expression in the pair of arrangements. The warm gray wall and bright white mantel supply a crisp, clean background that shows up flowers and art to best advantage.

The placement of objects on the mantel establishes a formal balance that suits the classic architectural details of the fireplace. The symmetry does not dictate matching arrangements, however. Rather, it serves as a framework within which the arrangements can express a similar spirit, yet assume individual personalities. This results in a more dynamic and interesting group.

Gently arching sprays of cotoneaster are inserted first to break the edge of the picture frame at each corner. Additional branches balance them, with the lower ones carrying the line below the edge of the

mantel. The branches define the shape of each arrangement by carving the space around it into voids, or negative spaces. These are repeatedly subdivided as flowers are inserted according to size, shape, color, and texture to create movement and depth in the design.

Long stems of blue violet delphiniums go in next for a strong statement of color that links the arrangement to the artwork. The tall spires are reinforced with lavender delphiniums. Then stems of cape plumbago are added. The dainty flowers of this subtropical shrub splash the design with pale blue, carrying the color quite low and out to the edges. Although the effect is delicate and airy, the flowers play an important part in strengthening the link between flowers, canvas, and porcelain figure.

The red, salmon, and magenta flowers are worked in next. Combining these crashing shades results in a warm, lively quality that complements the introspective mood and blue scheme of the painting. The contrast captures the eye and leads it into the picture plane along artfully constructed paths of color. Building the paths begins with the strongest tones. Vivid red zinnias are placed to the outside, where the bold color gives definition to the arrangements without overwhelming the art. Salmon-colored geraniums and roses occupy the place of honor. Inserting them at the rim of the container, facing away from the center, echoes the framing effect of the red flowers: The eye starts at the outside of each arrangement and moves in. Additional geraniums, roses, zinnias, and alstroemeria are then added to bring color through the design.

Marigolds, rosebuds, and zinnias are worked in next to introduce a note of yellow that brightens the deeper tones. It also pulls the yellow from the jars into the arrangement.

To finish, white pincushion chrysanthemums are drifted through the design on an upward course, highlighting the other flowers. With so much white in the setting, it is important to include a touch in the arrangements as well to tie them to the surroundings. The bright white also gives the compositions a crispness to match that of the room. Placing a book under each jar is a delightfully imaginative touch that adds character to the group.

Because the mouth of each jar is relatively small, the underpinnings for these arrangements require some special treatment. A water-soaked block of florist's foam wrapped in a plastic bag is wedged into the opening and the plastic is rolled down over the lip of the jar. The protruding chunk of foam is then covered with wire mesh, which is securely taped to the shoulder. This provides a larger working surface and allows stems to be inserted at low angles. The plastic bag helps keep the mechanics from being pushed down into the jar as the design is built up. It also protects old and valuable pieces from potential water damage.

Soft pastels of lavender, green, and yellow from K. Blackford's canvas find perfect expression in the flowers massed loosely on either side. Bold and bright against the massive stone chimney, the grouping is a startling and imaginative stroke in the rustic setting. The cool palette and light, refined quality of both flowers and painting refresh the warm tones and natural textures of wood and stone.

Developing the pair of arrangements begins outdoors on the worktable, where materials from field and garden are divided into two groups of equal amounts of each color and flower type. This assures that the finished designs will be similar. However, it is neither necessary nor desirable to make them identical. Twin arrangements tend to look stiff and unnatural.

Queen Anne's lace and flowers of fresh dill are the first materials inserted into the foam-packed brass compotes. The highest stems are placed slightly off-center to keep the compositions from being rigid. Additional stems define a fan shape. These lines are then reinforced and filled out with white snapdragons, feverfew chrysanthemums, phlox, and lizard's-tails. Apple green heads of hydrangea and sprigs of mint are added to give the design solidity. The strong note of green also intensifies the lavender tones.

The pink, lavender, and purple flowers are then worked into the design. Light pink snapdragons and dahlias go in first, followed by the red violet dahlias and pink yarrow. The deepest colors—magenta dahlias and carnations and purple phlox—are worked in last as accents. Finally, a single orange dahlia is tucked into each arrangement to pick up a thread of color in the upholstered chair. Coming from the warmer half of the color spectrum, the touch of orange also perks up the lavender scheme.

discerning eye can see the makings of something special in odds and ends left over from other arrangements. Three full garden roses, for example, inspire a lush, romantic design. An antique silver basket offers the appropriate note of elegance, and its soft sheen serves as the perfect foil for delicate colors. These flowers take on such a luminous quality against the dark canvas that the effect recalls the Baroque tradition of painting with dramatic contrasts of light and dark.

The three roses are inserted into the florist's foam first. The yellow rose is the largest and the only flower of its color in the group, so it naturally assumes primary importance. Framing it asymmetrically with the two peach roses gives it emphasis and plays up the basket handle as a feature in the design.

Star-of-Bethlehem goes in next. The stems of this imported flower assume sculptural curves that guide their best placement in the arrangement.

Bits of greenery are then added to enlarge and refine the shape sketched in by the flowers. A piece of spirea traces a feathery line that gives height. Basil flowers and the foliage of mandevilla, a subtropical vine, stretch the line to each side and forward. A fern and hosta leaves fill out the framework, and threadlike fruit clusters of sweet autumn clematis lighten the group with a fine, spidery texture.

The remaining flowers are then worked in to fill out the design and create a pleasing balance of colors. Garden roses, phlox, and the fragile-looking trumpets of mandevilla form a parabola of purplish pink that leads the eye through the composition. A peach gerbera daisy, additional roses, and tangerine miniature carnations are distributed throughout, their faces positioned to reinforce the feeling of movement. To finish, a white garden rose is tucked in low toward the rear, adding a soft highlight. Plumes of velvety blue sage accent the lines and soft colors and also give a sense of depth.

One splendid arrangement makes an immediate impact, and the mantel offers a choice location for such a display. Against the rich warmth of the oak paneling, the vibrant colors of these flowers shine with brilliance, making the arrangement the natural focal point of the room.

The design begins with elaeagnus and forsythia branches. These define a graceful, relaxed S-curve that stretches up to the overmantel molding and down below the shelf. Leucothoe is added to them for the counterbalancing diagonal that carries the eye from the mantel's edge up into the paneled area.

Dutch irises reinforce the primary vertical line and introduce a note of purple that intensifies the other colors. Freesias embellish the framework as well, adding a distinctive quality with their sharply angled stems and delicate, trumpetlike blossoms.

The arrangement is then filled in with tulips, narcissus, and ranunculuses worked in by color to create an intricate tapestry. The pink tulips accent the fluid, down-swept curves while the orange lily-flowering ones take center stage, accenting the primary line and drawing the eye toward the blue-and-white china on the mantel. Ranunculuses and narcissus are distributed evenly through the group for an overall impression of yellow with white highlights. The direction in which each flower faces reinforces the sense of movement through the design. Tucking some flowers in among the taller stems and turning flower faces to look to the rear also creates movement into and around the composition.

Three pink camellias are then inserted low and to the side of the arrangement, where they anchor the strong asymmetrical thrust. Glimpsed through other stems, the large, full flower faces draw the eye around the composition and give this side of the arrangement a pleasing view as well. Hyacinths at the container's edge accent the focal area and strengthen the effect of the irises. For the finishing touches, waxflower and heather fill voids and supply the contrasting scale and texture that add interest to the design.

A simple container is best for such an elaborate display. This one is a footed brass bowl filled with water-soaked florist's foam to receive the stems.

In a well-made marriage (*overleaf*) between container and flowers, each complements the other to create a perfect whole. The soft, delicate forms of Debutante camellias and the dainty blossoms of Paperwhite narcissus offer the right note of elegance for the French *blanc de chine* vase. By happy coincidence, the camellias are echoed in the fabric on the sofa. This link gives an impression of total harmony.

Because the flowers will be seen from above as well as from the eye level of someone seated on the sofa, the group must form a pleasingly full mass. To keep it from being too solid and hard, however, some flowers are recessed while others are made to protrude slightly. The largest blooms are placed to soften the rim of the vase all the way around. Two additional camellias round off the top of the low dome. Stems of narcissus are then inserted to loosen the shape and give a light, airy quality to the arrangement.

To prolong the life of the camellias, each stem is inserted in a florist's water vial. This is then secured in the small amount of florist's foam that rests on the bottom of the vase. The topmost leaves are also left on the stems, both to help draw the water to the flower and to hide the foundation.

A simple bouquet in a French mustard pot (*previous page*) adds a light-hearted touch to this breakfast table. The informality of the setting calls for nothing more complicated than a bunch of flowers. In spite of its apparent spontaneity, however, the arrangement is carefully composed. Glasses, napkins, and china give the cue for the pink theme, which is carried out with cactus dahlias, miniature roses, and chrysanthemums. Peegee hydrangea provides the contrasting note of bright green that heightens the impact of the pink flowers.

There are no underpinnings for this arrangement. Instead, the stems help hold each other in place. The lower flowers are positioned first to form a matrix that keeps the taller flowers where they are wanted. Achieving color balance and a pleasing mounded shape guides the placement of the blossoms.

Peegee hydrangea and a dahlia go in at the edge of the vase to soften it, and a few daisies carry the line below the container's rim. Queen Anne's lace gives height, loosening the outline with lacy flowers held on arching stems. Zinnias add bright highlights to the soft pink-and-green palette.

Wild ageratum, lantana, and a plume of blue sage supply the violet note that always enhances other colors. The lantana and sage also break the rounded shape to keep the arrangement from being too solid and tight. Tucking in one yellow dahlia blushed with pink repeats the yellow of the daisy's eye and perks up the group.

Although the arrangement has an artless, carefree look, the flowers require the same careful conditioning as those destined for more elaborate designs. Peegee hydrangea holds up well if the stems are split one inch and held in boiling water for thirty seconds, then placed in cold water overnight.

A favorite view bounded by a window can serve as a living canvas, against which flowers may be placed to bring a sense of the garden indoors. This arrangement is composed to embrace the bird feeder and the activity it brings.

Branches of myrtle and flowering cherry define a broad crescent that reaches up toward the bird feeder and down toward the floor. Additional branches embellish the shape. Keeping the downward-thrusting pieces on the left rather short gives the arrangement a feeling of stability without blunting its diagonal inclination.

A pair of red tulips goes in next, inserted fairly low to provide a focus. The petals are gently forced open to strengthen the impact of color. To prevent the flowers from forming a pair of "eyes," however, one is placed to look up and out, while the other faces in the direction of the crescent's descending line. Tucking the lower one back into the group also helps to prevent the disconcerting effect that a pair of large flowers can have.

Filling in the arrangement proceeds with heather, pink tulips, snapdragons, delphiniums, candytuft, and chrysanthemums. The spiky and pointed flowers fill out and reinforce the framework, adding the weight of color to the line materials. Because the heather is quite thick, the designer feathers it down by selectively scissoring off pieces to lighten the stem's appearance. Delphinium's two shades of blue pick up that color in the cachepot, so stems are positioned to carry it all the way through the design. To obtain a cleaner line, the designer trims some of the stalks by removing unwanted blossoms.

A large clump of candytuft adds strength to the focal area and softens the rim of the vase. Pink chrysanthemums and additional candytuft are then worked in to fill out the focal area and link it to the framework materials. Yellow pincushion chrysanthemums are added last to accent and highlight the crescent shape. Placing the highest stems to face the window underscores the feeling of depth.

To hold the materials at the desired cascading angles, florist's foam is mounded into the cachepot. Because adding water to the container may be difficult, a kitchen baster is used to top up the vase after the arrangement has been completed. On bright, sunny days, an arrangement in front of a window will show up primarily as a strongly backlighted silhouette. At night, however, the darkened window will serve as a foil for flowers gently illuminated by interior lights.

When flowers link up to some element in the immediate surroundings, the result is a completely satisfying harmony. Here three detail colors in the tablecloth find expression in a casual group of spring flowers. Because the tulips offer the largest shapes, they give the arrangement an overall impression of white. With their soft form and luminous quality, they imbue the arrangement with an air of fresh simplicity.

Native crabapple provides the initial framework. One vertical branch defines the axis, and a pair of diagonal branches establishes the width. Ranunculus buds reinforce and expand on this outline. Their twisting stems, chosen for the windblown quality they suggest, recall the blustery weather of early spring, and introduce into the composition another dimension of the season.

Next, the white tulips are positioned to follow the lines already established. Additional tulips also define a diagonal in opposition to that of the crabapple. Most of the stems are clipped fairly short so that the flowers do not stretch beyond the limits defined by the branches. This helps keep the tulips in proportion to the basket. To loosen the base of the design, however, one soft, chalicelike flower is allowed to fall below the container's edge.

The group is then filled in with tiny yellow and double-flowering narcissus, freesias, and fragrant pink daphne. The yellow narcissus form a garland of color through the arrangement, moving from low in front up to the crown and out to the side to carry the eye through the design. The sense of lively energy is subtly reinforced by the directions in which the flowers face. The stems are positioned so that some of the narcissus seem to look at the larger blossoms, while others look down at the base or into the depths of the group. Tucking the bright yellow blooms down into the arrangement where they can be glimpsed through the stems of the tulips also gives the group a feeling of dimension. Freesias and daphne counterbalance the yellows and bring the design forward.

To finish, boxwood sprigs are tucked in at the heart of the group, where the cool green color plays up the value of the white and yellow flowers. An arum lily leaf is placed to break the corner of the basket, softening the base of the design. A second leaf at the rear provides a backing, along with a few flowers which help ensure that the design will not look flat and unfinished if seen from this side.

A white wicker basket in the Chinese Chippendale style offers the appropriate light, summery feeling expressed by the flowers. A liner inside the basket holds the florist's foam and water.

A bay of floor-to-ceiling windows becomes the mise-en-scène for this formal architecture of flowers, which fills the space with soft color and lush texture. Although building such a pyramid requires a wealth of flowers, the process is facilitated by the use of a Waterford epergne as the foundation. Its two tiers provide readily accessible bases for the stems, and the crystal pedestal holds the composition aloft for a light, floating effect.

Branches of wild roses establish a fluid line that stretches high into the space of the bay window. The width is slightly more restrained, determined by the length of the flower stems available. It is defined with additional wild rose branches, which fall gracefully from the top tier. Mock orange reinforces the line. Along with thick bunches of wild roses, it is also tucked into the lower bowl, placed to cascade below the rim.

Building the arrangement proceeds with pink and white flowers positioned to radiate in all directions from the top tier. In the lower bowl, blossoms are pushed in close and placed to look up and out. Pink snapdragons and alstroemeria offer pointed forms that establish the pyramidal shape. The large face flowers are then positioned to give weight and fullness to the body of the group. Giant double peonies, roses, and camellias are inserted at varying depths to suggest movement in and out of the design. To accent the soft pinks, lavender and purple Dutch irises and delphiniums are worked in. The stems must be inserted carefully among the fragile camellias to avoid bruising them. The delphiniums and a starry wildflower called amsonia also embellish the shape, breaking the outline with their long, slender stems so that the arrangement looks full but not overstuffed or tight.

To finish, small bits of wild roses, variegated hosta, and Dainty Bess (a hybrid tea rose) are tucked in to cover the underpinnings. As a final touch, an orange tulip and a yellow-and-red one are added, enlivening the pinks.

Outfitting the epergne to receive this arrangement requires some special preparations. A chunk of florist's foam covered with wire mesh is secured to the top tier with strands of wire running under the bowl in both directions. The lower bowl is filled with blocks of foam, over which wire mesh is shaped and tied in place in a similar manner.

A boldly patterned background challenges the designer to choose flower colors and forms that can hold their own in the setting. In this powder room, red amaryllis easily becomes the cynosure. Its severe architectural quality expresses the same spirit as the French Régence appointments, and the enormous red flowers present an unbroken mass of color that stands up well against the black-and-white wallpaper.

The arrangement itself is the essence of simplicity. A single stalk of amaryllis fits snugly into the mouth of the vase, with daylily leaves slipped into one side to keep the columnar stem from looking too bare. Daylily leaves offer the same straplike shape as the foliage of the amaryllis, but are finer and smaller and in better proportion to the vase. Each amaryllis blossom may last three to four days if the hollow stalk is first filled with cool water and plugged with cotton before being placed in a water-filled container.

This Greek vase offers a suitably tall, clean shape for the amaryllis. It is stylistically appropriate as well, in that the decorative arts in the Régence period drew inspiration from ancient Greece and Rome.

*S*ummer's essence is concentrated in an armload of wildflowers massed in an antique copper pot. Although the arrangement has a loose, spontaneous quality, the design is worked with the same patient attention to color, line, and movement as is given to a more formal grouping of cultivated flowers. Such care is the key to its success as a lively, light-hearted design.

Shaping the bouquet begins with long, fluffy stems of black cohosh. Spiky but not stiff, these wildflowers are like fireworks, exploding from the center of the container. There are no mechanics other than the stems themselves, carefully positioned to hold each other in place.

Into this delicately balanced foundation, Queen Anne's lace, asters, and chicory are inserted to fill out the shape. Stems with a natural arch or curve are chosen for the base of the design, where they are needed to soften the edge of the vase.

The red and yellow flowers are added last. Red bee balm floats high in the arrangement at the outer edges of the fan shape, with just a few flower heads bringing the color low into the design. Blackberry canes loaded with wine-colored, unripe fruit add texture and interest. Most of the foliage is removed from the canes and bee balm to highlight their line and color.

The bright yellow faces of black-eyed Susans blaze like sunlight and must be handled carefully to keep them from overpowering the arrangement. The flowers are distributed loosely through the design, with stems radiating in the same manner as the cohosh. Positioning the flower faces to look to the side or upward at an angle not only reinforces the sense of movement, it also softens the impact of the color. Clustering a few blossoms to look forward takes full advantage of the strength of the yellow and helps lead the eye toward the center of the design.

These wildflowers require some special attention to last well in the arrangement. They should be cut very early in the morning before the dew has dried or late in the afternoon and immediately plunged into deep cool water. The bucket should be placed in the shade until the flowers can be conditioned.

*T*he welcoming effect of garden flowers and foliage is quite different from anything else. Here in the entry, maple leaves and goldenrod bring a sense of the season indoors, imbuing the arrangement with a sense of the life that exists in nature.

Maple and hemlock define the shape, which fills the corner with branches that reach up and forward. The lowest hemlock boughs stretch well below the rim of the container at an angle that recalls their natural down-swept habit of growth. Along with the forked, nearly bare maple limb that projects down to the edge of the console table, these branches give a fluid, graceful quality to the shape and serve to draw the eye up into the composition. Against the gold walls, the dark green hemlock also serves as a foil for the orange and apricot leaves and flowers. Knotweed and holly berries accent the line with additional layers of color and texture. The holly leaves are removed to accent the berries and to avoid too great a clutter of green that would detract from the orange.

Chrysanthemums, garden roses, and euphorbia then fill in with warm, rich colors keyed to those of the maple leaves. The most intense reds are concentrated at the heart of the arrangement. Salmon-colored chrysanthemums and red ones flushed with yellow fill out the body. Yellow, apricot, and pink flowers float at the outer edges, giving the group a light, airy quality. The chrysanthemums are used as they come from the flower shop, with multiple blossoms on each long stem. This strengthens the color value of each. The roses are also paired by color for greater impact.

Euphorbia streaks the arrangement with yellow, tracing a series of curves that provide a graceful counterpoint to the stiff chrysanthemums. Most of the leaves are removed to play up the sculptural quality of the stems.

For the finishing touch, goldenrod is worked into the front of the arrangement, giving fullness and depth to the heart of the design. A tall stem is also wedged carefully into the back of the group to strengthen the axis with a suggestion of substance.

The arrangement is built in a woven basket, which offers an informality in keeping with the character of the wildflowers and foliage. Because the basket is deep, it is filled with crumpled newspapers to raise the foundation high enough for flowers and branches to be inserted at acute angles. For the foundation, florist's foam is wrapped in foil, covered with wire mesh, and placed in a plastic liner which rests on the crumpled newspapers. Raising the basket on a carved stand gives the arrangement extra impact in the lofty entry.

An arrangement worked against a floral still life (*see also book jacket*) should express the same lavish elegance as the period painting. Here, imported flowers make it possible to anticipate spring and enjoy the luxury of tulips, roses, and lilacs before the last greenhouse-grown camellias of the season fade.

Lavender and white freesias give the height and width. The stiff stems, which terminate in acutely angled flower spikes, bring the line below the rim of the silver basket and beyond the edge of the sideboard. Additional stems begin the process of filling in the body. White ranunculuses reinforce the freesias. The succulent stems, which arch and bend to give an arrangement character, must reach deeply into the water-soaked florist's foam; otherwise, the flowers will not hold up well.

Apricot roses, orange and pink tulips, and bunches of white lilacs then fill in the shape. The unexpected combination of the orange hues with lavender and pink gives the group warmth and zest. The flowers are worked in around the center, which is kept free for the camellias. These are nearly the last materials to be added. To give dimension, one dark pink camellia is tucked in quite deep. A second lighter pink one is positioned low to the rear. White and pale pink camellias then fill in the place of honor across the base of the arrangement. Their insertion low and deep in the silver basket reinforces the impression of depth, and the large flower faces offer the eye a natural and pleasant place to rest. The glossy, dark green foliage is left on the foremost blossom to frame it and add weight to the focal area. Camellias tend to be fragile late in the season, so the flowers are discreetly wired for security with florist's wire passed through the base of each blossom and wrapped around the stems.

The design is finished with heather, which adds fullness at the crown and in the body. Bits of leucothoe are inserted at the rear to give the group a backing. A simple foundation of florist's foam fills the silver basket to receive the stems.

The wonderfully intense colors of these garden flowers seem to express the spirit of a sun-drenched summer day. Against the cool white wall, the brilliant palette shines with vivid clarity, offering a jubilant sense of welcome.

The object of such an arrangement is to embellish the furnishings, not overwhelm them. The group is therefore composed to fit the proportions of the chest and the Italian burl and gilded mirror. Working against the mirror requires the arrangement to have a good backing so that its reflection will be pleasing.

The design begins with a candelabrum-like branch of pink knotweed defining a tall line that stretches to the mirror's crest. White knotweed carries this line below the edge of the vase and across the mirror's apron. Additional branches bring the design forward for a frothy, three-dimensional quality.

A single foxtail lily is inserted next, paired with the pink knotweed, to strengthen the vertical line. Then the largest face flowers are worked in, carefully distributed through the arrangement to make sure they do not overpower the design. An orange garden lily and a vivid red hibiscus give the focus, while additional lilies carry color high in the arrangement. Bright green peegee hydrangea and feather-veined caladium leaves offer cool relief to these hot colors.

Smaller-stemmed flowers are then worked in to fill out the design and provide a rich balance of color. Zinnias, gerbera daisies, angel-wing begonias, and hosta (plantain lily) flowers supply tints and tones that intensify the red and orange flowers. The bright yellow marigolds, daisy chrysanthemums, and pincushion chrysanthemums are added next. The intensity of their color adds snap and freshness to the group, and the blossoms are positioned to draw the eye into the mirror. A few stems are worked into the opposite side of the arrangement for balance.

Arching stems of euphorbia are stripped of their leaves and inserted to accent the lines of the arrangement. Celosia serves as filler.

To finish, thick bunches of purple statice and stems of lily-of-the-Nile (agapanthus) are inserted toward the back of the design. The rich deep hue throws the warm colors into bold relief.

The container, a Chinese export wig stand, is appealing in its own right. Its colors relate to the flowers but do not compete with them. Florist's foam projects above the rim of the container so that flowers and branches can be inserted at low angles. Carefully placed accessories are the final touches that bring out the total harmony of the group, integrating the flowers into the setting.

The imported flower that gives this arrangement its dynamic character is foxtail lily. Also known as desert candles, the spiky racemes are like exclamation points. Mixing them with other florist's materials and plants from the garden and roadside produces a lively quality that recalls European window boxes crowded with masses of blooms.

The composition begins with foxtail lilies defining several broad crescents. The overlapping shapes cradle the painting on the far wall and draw the eye to it.

Knotweed and pokeberry are added next. These materials reinforce the foxtail lilies and carry the line below the base of the arrangement. Although many people look upon pokeberry as an unsightly weed, certain English flower arrangers prize its black berries, which bring a strong note of contrast to a group of flowers. The ripe fruit falls and shatters easily, however. For this composition, the branches were cut before the berries ripened, and the leaves were removed to reveal slender, glossy stems that shade from purple to green.

With the framework in place, the face flowers are added. Chrysanthemums, dahlias, zinnias, rubrum lilies, and roses look up, out, or down, radiating from the heart of the design.

Color leads the eye through the arrangement as well. Red chrysanthemums and rubrum lilies, bunched by type, are placed to balance each other. Massing these flowers strengthens the impact of their color and links the design to the rich red walls. Soft peach roses, salmon-colored dahlias, and yellow chrysanthemums bring forward those colors in the painting. The bright yellow also accents the foxtail lilies and highlights the form of the design. Euphorbia and miniature gladiolus provide the finishing brushstrokes with out-and-down lines, and lily-of-the-Nile supplies the essential touch of blue that intensifies the other colors.

The container for this arrangement is a carved wooden relic box with four angels forming sturdy legs. The box communicates stability in contrast to the energy of the design; it also lifts the flowers for a more fluid, graceful effect.

Gloriosa daisies have such a distinctive personality that they define the character of the whole group of flowers, giving the bouquet the feeling of a country garden. Blending an informal look with the refinement of this setting is accomplished with a contemporary metal container that both lifts the composition and defines its form.

Ivy and orange dahlias define the circumference of the arrangement. To loosen the shape while retaining the sense of roundness, the flowers are made to project freely beyond the circular frame. A piece of ivy brings the line forward as well. To obtain the desired curve, the stem is turned so that the underside of the leaves is uppermost.

Spiky stems of delphinium reinforce the three-dimensional framework, which is then filled in with a wealth of garden flowers. Roses, zinnias, gerbera daisies, geraniums, and gloriosa daisies are worked in by color to assure a rich balance of warm, summery hues. The flowers with the greatest visual weight are inserted to extend below the container, where they define the lower edge of the circle. Ordinarily a chalk white blossom would not be considered visually heavy; however, the size of this dahlia and its brilliant contrast with the warm colors give it the importance and impact needed at the base of the design.

To finish, Queen Anne's lace and white daisy chrysanthemums are added. They supply highlights and balance the effect of the dahlia. Lavender ageratum accents the color scheme.

The foliage is left on the roses, ageratum, and geraniums to help hide the underpinnings. The leaves also form voids that help play up the importance of the individual flowers and keep the design from looking overstuffed.

A block of florist's foam wedged into the bowl at an angle assists the development of a rounded outline. Wire mesh is molded over the foam and the whole is taped to the bowl to hold it securely.

An arrangement on the coffee table is necessarily small, and building it in the round does not require a large collection of materials. It does demand patience, however, because each angle must present a different, appealing view.

The small brass compote calls for dainty greenery. Petite English ivy is used to establish the circumference, with sprigs inserted to reach toward the table at different angles. This keeps the arrangement from becoming boxy.

Chrysanthemums further define the shape. Those with bright orange faces mark the crown and outside edges. The vivid red chrysanthemums and roses, which are visually heavy, are tucked in close. Positioning the flowers so that they seem to radiate from a central point gives each view a place for the eye to rest. At the same time, some of the flowers can be seen in profile, which moves the eye around the composition.

To avoid a dense, pincushion effect, some of the flower faces are recessed snugly into the group and others are pulled forward. The pointed shapes of ornamental peppers and pink rosebuds and the linear quality of the stems of globe amaranths also help break the outline, keeping it from being tight and uniform. Following the pattern established by the chrysanthemums, the most vivid flowers are tucked in close, while the lightest-colored flowers float at the outside edges, giving an airier quality to the group.

Cornflowers supply the note of blue that gives depth to the other colors. Adding the pink nerine lilies and freesias and lavender liatris lightens and relieves the intensity of the scheme. The combination of discordant shades also adds an unexpected liveliness.

To finish, threads of hemlock are tucked in, softening the outline. Ivy fills gaps, hiding the florist's foam and creating cool voids that are as important to the design as the flowers themselves.

Garden roses will last longer and be easier to handle if the thorns are first removed from the bottom half of the stems. This improves the flowers' ability to take up water. Removing every other leaf also aids in water absorption, and it lightens the appearance of the flowers.

Foliage, Flowers, and the Seasons

Flowers bring a sense of the garden indoors, breathing life into a room as nothing else does. Roses and pineapple sage evoke the casual, easy feeling of summer with loose, relaxed lines and soft, full flowers that give the design an airy grace.

The three velvety red roses are the most important flowers, so they begin the arrangement. The two largest ones are placed at the eye level of someone seated on the sofa or a nearby chair. The third large rose lifts the eye slightly to a fourth, still in bud. A barely open gerbera daisy carries a touch of red to the back of the arrangement for a sense of depth.

Pineapple sage is added next, distributed through the arrangement so that the stems seem to radiate from a single point. The leaves are removed along most of the length of each stem to play up the slender red flowers and the beaded effect of the line. Arching and stretching from the heart of the arrangement, the sage imparts an ethereal quality to the group.

Galax leaves then fill out the design, creating the effect of a glossy green carpet above which the roses float. White, pink, and yellow roses finish the arrangement, adding highlights and depth.

Glass containers normally require light, airy arrangements that do not depend on florist's foam, as it would show through the glass. In this case, however, florist's foam was wedged onto a needlepoint holder in the bottom of the broad bowl, then effectively obscured by the mound of galax leaves. The greenery recedes and lifts the arrangement, giving it a sense of buoyancy.

Galax leaves will last a very long time if they are immersed in cold water when first cut. After thirty minutes, they should be placed upright in cold water until they are to be used.

Combinations (*overleaf*) of fruit and vegetables with flowers and branches create a lush effect with rich layers of color and form. When the flowers are fall-blooming and the branches are berry-laden, they infuse the group with a harvest theme that celebrates the earth's fecundity.

Construction begins with the pineapple, which is anchored to the underpinnings with wooden florist's picks to hold it at the desired angle. Branches of bittersweet are inserted next. These balance the thrust of the pineapple with vigorous curves that sweep through the design, emerging on the opposite end with an almost aggressive energy.

Acorn squash, an eggplant, lemons, oranges, bananas, and red and green apples are then mounded in the bowl. Wooden florist's picks hold some of the fruit in place, including the grapes, whose stems are wired to the picks. To suggest an overflowing abundance, the green grapes are draped to break the edge of the bowl.

Garden-grown chrysanthemums and globe amaranths are then worked into pockets left among the vegetables and fruit. Grouping the flowers by color gives each hue greater impact and draws the eye through the arrangement along overlapping paths. The largest rust red flower faces go in low, softening the edge of the bowl and arching gently below the base of the arrangement to loosen the design. A few stems of pokeberry are also worked in along with the flowers. Usually overlooked as a roadside weed, this plant offers vivid red violet stems and glossy purple black berries that spice the arrangement with a note of surprise.

To finish, clusters of gold-dust aucuba and parsley are tucked in at the bowl's edge, further softening the base of the design. The parsley's deep green foliage also initiates a path of color, leading the eye through the grapes and beyond to the pineapple foliage.

The arrangement is built upon a low foundation of water-soaked florist's foam to give a base for the flower stems and branches. Fruit that is simply placed in the bowl without florist's picks can be eaten later when the arrangement is dismantled.

Clustering them near the crown intensifies the impact of color. Tendrils of ivy are inserted to trail down the sides of the vases and to stretch into the surrounding space, supplying dimension. Coppery nandina berries introduce a variation on the form of the grapes and add seasonal interest to the design.

To finish, ivy, pears, kiwifruit, and pomegranate halves are artfully arranged on the table at opposite ends of the group. For a holiday table, colored candles may replace the standard ivory or white candles. Here rose pink candles pick up the theme of the flowers and pineapples. The colors in the Herend Queen Victoria china are also integrated into the scheme, giving the whole a pleasing unity.

Gleaming brass and silver, gilt-edged French crystal, and soft candlelight (*previous page and above*) set the stage for a splendid evening. In keeping with the spirit of the occasion, fruit and flowers are heaped in brass vases to provide sumptuous points of interest on the table. However, they are kept low enough for guests to converse comfortably across them.

Pink roses from the garden and two ornamental pineapples from the florist suggested the dominant color scheme, with bright green and deep purple as accents and yellow as a highlight.

To achieve the effect of bowls brimming with fruit, glass liners are set into the brass vases and mounded with florist's foam. Wire mesh covers the foam to form the foundation on which the arrangements are built.

The vases are composed one at a time. The second is intended to mirror the first but not to duplicate it precisely. The ornamental pineapples are the largest element and so are positioned first, secured to the foam base with wooden florist's picks. The distinctive form and texture of the pineapples give character to the arrangements, and placing them at opposing angles suggests a wide crescent that visually links the two vases into a single composition.

Constructing each arrangement then proceeds from the bottom up. Clusters of purple, green, and red grapes cascade over both sides of the container, held in place with wooden florist's picks. Pears, limes, lemons, carambolas, Oriental persimmons, and apples are massed around these, distributed to achieve a rich balance of color. Kiwifruit and pomegranates, cut into halves to display their internal patterns and colors, go in near the top of the mound of fruit.

Flowers, ivy, and nandina berries are worked in last. The flowers—roses, alstroemeria, nerine lilies, and chrysanthemums—are inserted into florist's water vials filled with water before being tucked into the design.

Artistry with flowers springs from a lively awareness of the beauty inherent in each plant's form. When that form is presented in an unexpected way, it gives a startling, fresh character to the whole group.

The flower clusters of mahonia have that effect here. When all of the leaves are removed from the stems, the stiff racemes look like flowers from another world.

The arrangement begins with slender branches of quince defining an open, graceful outline. Winter honeysuckle, Japanese andromeda, and the mahonia flower clusters embellish this skeletal shape and bring the line below the rim of the container. Long stems of Japanese andromeda supply additional weight to the outline, while short pieces help hide the underpinnings and soften the edge of the vase. Nippon lily (*Rohdea japonica*) berries are positioned next, deeply recessed to give an impression of color inside the arrangement.

Into this framework of greenery and branches go the flowers, a collection of odds and ends from the garden and florist. Yellow freesias serve as a bridge in the outline between the topmost stem of mahonia and a lower one. Yellow and orange ranunculuses carry the note of bright color through the design. Narcissus brings the white from the container into the arrangement, and delphiniums, a few camellias, anemones, and a single Lenten rose are added to achieve a balance of colors and forms.

Red tulips give unity to this varied assortment, defining a graceful sweep of color that arches in opposition to the upturned quince. Additional tulips carry the eye from below the vase up into the rear of the design.

Composed in an English loving cup filled with florist's foam, the arrangement is lifted on a carved stand to emphasize its light, ethereal quality.

*H*ospitality begins in the foyer, where an armload of chrysanthemums and fall foliage promises a warm welcome from a gracious hostess. The backbone of the arrangement is a rugged huckleberry limb. Its jagged, irregular shape reaches high into the space defined by the sweep of the stairs, offering a line in proportion to the setting.

Dogwood branches, cattails, firethorn (pyracantha), and zebra grass are inserted to define the skeleton, which is then fleshed out with chrysanthemums, celosia, and waxflower. The lighter-colored flowers are worked in first, followed by successively darker tones, to form interconnected paths of color that keep the eye traveling through the design. To convey a sense of movement in and out of the arrangement, some stems are pulled far forward, while others are pushed back into the design. A few tall stems are also worked in among the grasses. These tallest chrysanthemums need some encouragement to remain upright; the stems are encircled with a length of florist's wire fastened around the huckleberry limb.

Three proteas are grouped low in the arrangement, suggesting a sense of weight that subtly defines the focal point. Finally, for a note of surprise that adds spice to the composition, a long stem from a banana pepper plant is inserted to trail from the base of the design. The leaves and surplus branches have been removed to play up the shape and colors of the peppers, which are in various stages of maturity from green to red.

Building a large arrangement with a number of coarse-stemmed materials requires sturdy mechanics. Large blocks of florist's foam are packed into the bronze liner that fits inside the top of the urn. The foam projects well above the container to permit stems to be inserted at low angles. To keep the foam from breaking apart under the weight of so many stems, wire mesh is taped securely over it. No special measures are required to hide the mechanics, because the canopy of face flowers effectively screens it from view.

*B*ringing the beauty and freshness of flowers to a chairside table breathes life into a small, specific environment. Here a mixture of florist's flowers and garden materials are combined in a copper vase for a simple bouquet that complements the comfortable, unpretentious setting.

Azalea and holly olive branches are inserted into the florist's foam first. Foliage is lightly pruned from some of the azalea branches to enhance the arching stems, which give the group an airy quality.

Dense clusters of holly berries are inserted next, balancing the azalea branches. The foliage is removed to emphasize the still-green fruit, which gives character to the group. A long corkscrew curl of bittersweet is also added, providing unexpected line.

One large dahlia is then placed off-center, just above the mouth of the vase, to give the arrangement a "bosom" when seen from this side. Carnations stretch below the rim and up to the lamp, completing the framework. Filling in with color proceeds with dahlias, chrysanthemums, roses, and miniature carnations.

To assure a balanced distribution, the colors are worked in one at a time, starting with lavender and pink and moving to the reds, rusts, and yellows. The red dahlias give the eye a resting place when the arrangement is viewed from the chair. The color also picks up that of the mat on the painting above, bridging the gap between flowers and setting. Because the reds are visually strong, they are positioned in a triangle to suggest stability. To keep the triangle from being too hard or obvious, however, the flowers that form the apex are placed at the back, facing the wall. These and other stems added to the back of the design form a "bustle" that gives the arrangement dimension. Finally, the arrangement is given a more finished appearance by being placed on a plain black stand near a spouted vessel from Peru.

Ordinary apples, pears, and lemons are indispensable to traditional holiday decorations. But when piled in a silver tureen with an eggplant, dried ornamental pineapples, and pink poinsettias, they become part of a very untraditional but dramatic centerpiece for a holiday buffet supper.

The poinsettias and a brightly patterned table runner suggested a color scheme in harmony with the persimmon walls and draperies, so fruit and flowers were chosen to grade from pale pink to bright red to deep purple, with green and yellow materials added for highlight and contrast.

Pear branches pruned from the garden establish the lines, which sweep up toward the ceiling and out toward each end of the table, drawing the silver candlesticks into the composition. A pair of ornamental pineapples, dried to a soft pink, are inserted next at angles that balance those of the branches. Eggplant is also positioned at this point, secured to the florist's foam with wooden florist's picks. Because the eggplant and pineapple are the largest fruit used, they are fixed at the desired angles early in the process. Apples, pears, and clusters of purple grapes, also attached to florist's picks, are then worked in around the eggplant

and pineapples. Lemons, held in place by toothpicks, rest on the larger fruit, and short, thick spikes of red berries from Nippon lily (*Rohdea japonica*) help fill out the arrangement. To hide the underpinnings and echo the rich tones of the eggplant and grapes, mahogany-colored Fraser photinia and cross vine are tucked in around the base.

The last step is to add the poinsettias. To keep them fresh, the stem ends are singed with a candle flame, then inserted in florist's water vials. With this treatment, they should last about a week.

Although the fruit appears to fill the tureen, actually it is piled on a foundation of florist's foam which projects slightly above the rim of the container. This way a generous mound can be assembled with a small amount of fruit, and foliage can be inserted at low angles to soften the edge of the tureen. To give the heavy fruit a sturdy support, the foam is covered with wire mesh, which is tied with fine wire to the handles of the tureen. The foliage effectively conceals the wire.

nusual plant materials from the garden can transform a group of lovely but otherwise predictable spring flowers into an extraordinary composition. The thorny branches of hardy orange (*Poncirus trifoliata*) look quite wicked, but along with the red flower spikes of red buckeye and branches of white redbud, the plant infuses the group with an exciting, natural quality that few purchased materials can match.

Establishing the formal fan shape begins with bridal wreath spirea, winter honeysuckle, and red buckeye. The buckeye limbs are stripped of most leaves to emphasize the flower spikes, which are used freely here because they harmonize so well with the flesh pink tones in the Hadley Worcester urn.

White quince and azalea branches with the flowers still in bud go in next, following the contours of the fan and bringing the design forward. Two large branches of hardy orange are then wedged in place toward the back of the group, where they trace rugged silhouettes against the wall. This linear quality is important to the effect of the arrangement, so it is essential that it have a clean background uncluttered by patterned walls or other plant materials. To avoid a

rigid regularity that could suggest "ears," the two branches are inserted at different angles and staggered depths.

With most of the woody materials in place, the flowers are then worked in to fill the body of the design with color. Anemones, tulips, and freesias elaborate on the red theme established by the red buckeye, and groups of daffodils and Lenten roses at the mouth of the vase lighten the effect of the bolder flowers. Daffodils are also worked into the back of the arrangement, forming points of yellow that can be seen through the stems. This technique, used with the anemones and tulips as well, increases the composition's interest by giving it a feeling of depth.

For the finishing touch, tall branches of white redbud are wedged in to give a taller, more graceful line and to brighten the top of the arrangement. The deep gray bark of the redbud also provides a note of contrast that enhances the outline. An additional bit of redbud is tucked in low at the front to balance the effect of the daffodils.

The foundation of water-soaked florist's foam has wire mesh crumpled over it, and it is taped to the urn for security. Using the lid as an accessory supplies a satisfying finished look.

daisies from the garden, roses, miniature carnations, cockscomb celosia, and statice.

To establish a natural resting place for the eye, face flowers of similiar size but different colors are blended skillfully. Concentrating the lavender Michaelmas daisies and daisy chrysanthemums low in the design and highlighting them with white chrysanthemums and yellow roses give the needed sense of mass and importance to the "bosom" of the arrangement. A rich carmine rose tucked deep into the base adds depth and weight.

Additional Michaelmas daisies and chrysanthemums carry the lavender theme through the design. Working in the deeper tones of metallic pink carnations, burgundy cockscomb, and rusty red chrysanthemums intensifies the pastels; deep yellow pincushion chrysanthemums and three orange rosebuds supply points of bright color to lighten the whole group.

To finish, the epergne's two side cups are mounded with miniature carnations, statice, and chrysanthemums. Framing the arrangement with a pair of brass and Venetian glass candlesticks completes the composition and brings the delicate, shimmering quality of the chandelier down to the table.

The dining-room table is the natural choice for a place to display flowers that will suggest a sense of occasion. To fill the lofty space created by the vaulted ceiling, the arrangement must assume grand proportions without becoming too heavy for the subtle refinement of the setting. This formal architecture of flowers, built up in a footed brass epergne, meets the need. By restricting the materials to finely textured foliage and small to medium-size flowers, the designer has captured a light, airy quality that complements the crystal chandelier and the exquisite handwoven scarf from the Far East.

Beginning with the center container of the epergne, a soft, feathery outline is established with long, supple branches of serissa. This shrub propagates readily and can stand heavy pruning. A pair of stems gives the height, leading the eye into the chandelier. Lower branches arch broadly to each side and forward to create a loose, fluid framework. Short pieces of pachysandra are inserted next, covering the florist's foam and giving solidity to the center of the design.

With the greenery in place, spiky stems of miniature gladiolus and alstroemeria are inserted to embellish the shape defined by the branches. The arrangement is then built up with chrysanthemums, Michaelmas

The artlessness of a few flowers evokes a private world of simple pleasures. An imported flower, star-of-Bethlehem, offers a clean, sculptural quality that refreshes this desktop collection. The delicate blossoms cluster on spikes that curl like kittens' tails, inviting a closer look to appreciate the whimsy of their form.

Creating a pleasing asymmetrical balance is a matter of letting the posture of each flower suggest its placement in the vase. The stair-step line gives the effect of flowers bursting out of the vase with an energy that begins in the undulating outline of the container. The snug fit in the vase's small mouth allows the stems to hold each other at the desired height.

Three leaves of Chinese evergreen, a houseplant, collar the stems, and a single leaf of hosta softens the edge of the vase. The broad foliage suggests a sense of presentation and provides a comfortable weight to anchor the flowers.

In an arrangement of few flowers, the vase becomes an important part of the composition. This one provides interest through its sharp contrast with the aggressive line of the stems. At the same time, a subtle harmony exists between its bulbous, double-gourd shape and the form of the flower clusters.

With a tree-shaded slope for a backdrop (*previous page*), this lavish display brings the outdoors inside. Fall foliage and flowers from the garden and roadside set the seasonal tone. The florist's year-round varieties carry out the theme.

The outline of the arrangement is defined with branches that announce the time of year with a mixture of red and bronzy green leaves. Cotoneaster, spirea, bittersweet, and zebra grass elaborate on the triangular shape.

Peach gladiolus are then positioned to carry a strong note of color high into the arrangement. Inserting the gladiolus early is important, because the thick stems would be difficult to put in later after the mechanics have become crowded with stems. Gerbera daisies and lilies are added next for the same reason. Placing the red gerbera daisies and yellow lilies demands careful attention to color balance because these two are so dominant.

With the large flowers in place, the smaller-stemmed blossoms can be worked in. These include Michaelmas daisies, alstroemeria, roses, chrysanthemums, and miniature gladiolus. As with the larger flowers, they are inserted one color at a time to ensure balance and to create a pleasing flow from red, orange, and peach to gold and yellow. Lavender, pink, and white are used as highlights. Recessing some of the face flowers strengthens the impression of warm color and implies depth. Allowing other stems to lean far forward or to stretch to the sides gives a loose, airy effect that keeps the design from being stiff.

To fill in, white hardy begonias, hosta leaves, and purple statice are added. These hide the mechanics and give solidity to the center of the arrangement. Spirea and dogwood branches go in around the base to provide undershadow. In addition, they serve as a ''bustle'' at the back of the arrangement to keep it from looking flat. The delicate, lacy lines traced by the spirea also repeat the spilling-over quality of the outline and subtly link the mass of flowers to the table.

Building an arrangement of this size requires stepping back occasionally to check for holes, balance, and correct proportion. After a final scrutiny, two stems of goldenrod are added to extend the design still higher for better relationship to the window wall. Using two stems avoids the pitfalls of a stiff apex or too-thin crown, which can result when a single branch defines the top of the arrangement.

A pedestal vase gives the needed lift for greatest impact. Placing the vase on a scrolled stand is an extra touch that conveys a sense of presentation. The stand also supplies visual weight to help anchor the group.

The basic goal of Japanese-style flower art is to reproduce nature's beauty within the confines of the container. This is accomplished with an extreme economy of materials, yielding a terse composition that invites contemplation.

The arrangement begins with a wisteria branch whose bent and twisting line suggests a sense of life and growth. In contrast to the elastic tension in its climbing form, the weeping chains of flowers create an aura of tranquility. The branch is wedged onto the needlepoint holder toward the rear so that the flowers will hang just beyond the edge of the bronze container, producing a sense of dimension.

The arum lily leaves are then positioned at the base of the branch to provide transition between the wisteria and the container. The leaves are kept low to ensure a subtle and understated effect. One leaf is placed to face forward to help balance the weight of the flowers. Inserted at an angle, it reinforces the crook of the branch and repeats the strong diagonal of the new leaves unfolding behind the flower clusters, creating unity within the design. Turning the other leaves in profile plays up their wavy contours and subdues the impact of their color.

In an art as precise as *ikebana*, even the position of the antique bronze container is important. Both mushroom handles should be visible to create a pleasing balance. The mechanics rest to one side at the back of the bowl, so that the branch can move diagonally through the space thus defined.

Wisteria will last well if the branch is slit at the bottom to a depth of about one inch and inserted in hot tap water for fifteen to twenty minutes before being placed in deep, cool water overnight. Arum lily leaves hold up quite well if submerged in cool water for twenty-four hours before being arranged.

lmost any decorative object that can receive a bowl to hold water can become the starting point for an arrangement of flowers. This Chinese wedding basket offers the ideal foundation for a design that plays up to the painting on the far wall.

A single hawthorn branch is wedged firmly in place first to establish the line. Unwanted leaves, twigs, and even a secondary branch are trimmed off for a lighter, cleaner shape. Additional hawthorn brings the main line forward over the edge of the basket and fills out the framework.

Euphorbia is inserted next to reinforce and fill out the line. Because the foliage of this flower usually gives a messy look and detracts from the sculptural quality of the stems, it is removed here. The plant bleeds a milky sap, so stripping the leaves is usually done when the flowers are reconditioned, allowing time for the stem cuts to seal.

With the skeleton established, the gerbera daisies are worked into the design, followed by the geraniums. In each case, the tallest stems are placed to emphasize the upward thrust of the main branch, echoing its rhythms of growth with their own springing lines. As sinuous stems overlay jagged branches, gaps or negative spaces are created. These produce the light, airy quality that gives the design character. The gaps are filled with additional shorter stems only to the extent necessary to keep the design from seeming spotty or empty. Intermediate stems carry color forward and beyond the baseline, and the shortest flowers provide "bosom" and depth.

Yellow pincushion chrysanthemums are added last to brighten and lighten the scheme. Most of the yellow buttonlike blooms project above the other flowers, loosening the outline. For depth, a few of them are pushed into the arrangement.

Aucuba and geranium leaves finish off the group. The leaves soften the edge of the basket and provide an undershadow that serves as a visual anchor for the soaring main branch.

To support the physical weight of the arrangement, a plastic plant saucer sits on the top level of the three-tiered wedding basket, holding a chunk of florist's foam. This is covered with wire mesh, which is secured to the edges of the basket with florist's wire.

esigners who observe their gardens carefully through the year (*overleaf*) develop a sensitivity to the personality of each season. Expressing this spirit in their arrangements becomes a working philosophy that guides their choice and use of materials. Autumn brings to mind golden light and flaming colors. This outdoor arrangement interprets the essence of that season with a seemingly spontaneous collection of branches and florist's flowers gathered into a large basket.

Branches of dogwood and maple go in first to define a loose fan shape. This is reinforced with elaeagnus, Nellie R. Stevens holly, and hemlock. Although the group is designed to be seen primarily from the front, branches also fill out the rear to keep it from being flat. Nandina canes and peegee hydrangea are positioned next. The coppery berry clusters and large, soft flower heads provide masses of muted color inside the design and carry it well below the basket's rim, giving a lush, expansive quality to the shape. To play up the sculptural lines of the longer stems, most of the leaves are removed.

With the woody stemmed materials in place, the flowers fill in the shape. Celosia, gerbera daisies, liatris, and chrysanthemums are grouped by color rather than dotted about; this strengthens the impact of each. Weaving the colors together to form a bright autumn tapestry requires attention to balance, transition, and accent. Repetition helps achieve balance, and the palette itself assures transition. The juxtaposition of contrasting colors yields accents.

To give the overall design warmth, the red and yellow chrysanthemums are concentrated near the center. For balance, notes of red and yellow are then repeated in the composition. The orange flowers are placed so that they seem to emanate from the two primary colors at the nucleus, providing transition and enhancing the warm effect. Pink gerbera daisies pick up the hue of the hydrangea. Liatris gives depth to the pastels and intensifies the yellow flowers. In such a large arrangement, it is useful to leave the main stems of branching chrysanthemums intact so that the multiple blossoms will provide a large splash of color.

Finishing the group is a matter of filling voids with irises and geraniums. Because there are only three stems of irises, they are grouped together for a stronger value of blue. The geraniums provide bright color near the focus. Their foliage serves as filler and helps to soften the edge of the basket.

To provide the underpinnings for the arrangement, blocks of water-soaked florist's foam are wrapped in heavy foil and placed inside the basket. The top of the foam is exposed to receive the stems.

A mantel (*previous page*) presents an excellent platform on which to build an arrangement. The shelf permits the designer to make liberal use of long branches that stretch and fall in expansive, overspreading curves. These convey a quality of unstudied natural beauty and languid easy grace. Generally flowers should not cover a painting, but in this case the canvas is so dark that it serves as a frame for the body of the design. Against the nearly black background, the flowers are thrown into sharp relief.

Elaeagnus defines the upright line that projects across the painting and the horizontals that break the edge of the mantel. The upright stem is turned to show its silvery underside, which gleams against the dark canvas. Winter honeysuckle and Florida leucothoe elaborate on the shape. To emphasize the linearity of the leucothoe and to lighten its impact, leaves are selectively pruned from the branches.

Forsythia reinforces and balances the elaeagnus and continues its diagonal thrust below the mantel's edge. Hemlock then goes in low at the base to give weight to the foundation and to soften the edge of the mantel.

Camellias are positioned next. With stems inserted in florist's water vials, they are clustered low in the arrangement, concealing the container and providing a natural resting place for the eye.

The remaining flowers are then worked in to integrate the line with the focus. Both color and flower type contribute to the decisions on placement. Yellow lilies, coral gladiolus, and white snapdragons are tall and spiky, so they reinforce the crown and the horizontal lines. Flowers with good faces or fine textures fill in through the body of the design and provide a balanced distribution of color. Tulips, anemones, ranunculuses, carnations, and gerbera daisies carry out the theme of pink and red, accented with orange and yellow ranunculuses.

To help balance the effect of the white camellias at the heart of the group, white spider chrysanthemums and candytuft are then worked in. The most muted pinks, provided by Scotch broom, a rosebud, and gladiolus, frame the focus.

For the finishing touches, delphiniums are added. They give the note of violet that enhances the other colors. Thick bunches of heather are also inserted, embracing the focal area and reinforcing the design's overspreading curves.

For this arrangement, the container is a simple metal vessel from which florist's foam projects by several inches. This allows material to be inserted at low angles to create a cascading line.

The art of using flowers as natural ornaments rests on keying the materials to some note in the room. Here, flowers pick up the note of pink in the sofa fabric and complement its muted green and that of the tablecloth. A bronze Chinese container with a dragon pedestal suggests an open, linear arrangement in the Oriental manner.

The design begins with a single branching spire of quince wedged onto the needlepoint holder. Positioned toward the rear to form the backbone, its natural curves relieve the jagged stiffness of the outline. The secondary branches supply energy and movement, jutting at angles to divide the surrounding space. To balance the upward tension of this line, a forked and thorny branch softened with fragile blossoms is inserted at the base. A third small branch bridges the two, completing the framework that leads the eye toward the sofa.

An elegant specimen camellia is then inserted where these lines meet, giving the focus. A pair of leaves is left on the stem to help frame the flower face. To strengthen its impact further, a fatsia leaf is tucked in behind it, angled to play up the camellia and anchor the design.

Ranunculuses are then worked in to fill out the group. Chosen for their perfect reflection of the camellia and quince colors, they also offer flower forms compatible with that of the camellia, giving a sense of unity to the arrangement. Their twisting, supple stems stretch and bend, bringing color below the vase to soften its edge. Tall stems carry the pink-and-white theme up into the design toward the quince blossoms. To gain depth, some of the ranunculus faces are placed to look toward the side or rear, moving the eye around the arrangement. Most of the finely cut foliage is scissored off to emphasize the linear quality of the stems. Leaves that are not removed serve as filler, softening the spaces with a light green filigree.

For the final touch, the bronze vase is placed on a red lacquer base. This gives the arrangement a sense of presentation, and the color ties the group to the accessories and the note of orange in the sofa fabric.

inking flowers to some special feature of a room can yield delightful results. The inspiration here is a window wall that divides a curtain of evergreens into a series of living canvases. Displaying an arrangement of mixed flowers against one of these draws the outdoor tapestry into the composition of flowers, sofa, table, and accessories. The rustic texture of the vine basket is a visual reference to the woodsy surroundings and suits the comfortable informality of the room.

Long branches of greenery establish an expansive base on which to build the composition. Elaeagnus and Japanese maple, inserted at opposing angles, mark the top of the arrangement. The line begun by the elaeagnus then sweeps through the design, emerging in an extravagant arc of grapevine. The maple branch begins a broad curve which ends in a flourish of maple leaves. These lower leaves soften the edge of the basket and bring the objects on the table into the composition. Additional maple, elaeagnus, grapevine, and hemlock elaborate on the main lines. To give the elaeagnus more prominence against the green backdrop, some of the branches are turned to show the silvery underside. Sprays of hemlock are also reversed to make use of their blue green color.

The pointed, stiff, and heavy flowers are inserted next. Because of their distinctive character, they are best used to embellish the skeleton of greenery. They also rough in the paths of color that will create movement through the design.

A trio of foxtail lilies marks the crown of the arrangement. Repeating the angles of the greenery, they assert an asymmetrical balance that leads the eye toward the table. Stalks of magic lilies reflecting the accent color of the pink pillow are then positioned to descend gradually into the design. Panicles of hydrangea go in next, forming a low arc across the basket. Allowing one large cluster to fall below the bottom of the basket prevents a rigid baseline and reinforces the grapevine. Snipping off the large leaves from the stems heightens the impact of the dense white flower heads. Finally, feathery plumes of dark pink astilbe are added. These spread out in a fan shape that counterbalances the arrangement's asymmetrical thrust. To keep the fan from being rigid, one stem of astilbe angles down toward the table, another points toward the back of the design, and a third inclines slightly forward. This placement also underlines the three-dimensional quality of the arrangement.

Developing the group then proceeds by building up layers of color to achieve a balanced mix. Because the green background is relatively dark, the lighter tints are placed at the perimeter to help throw the design

81

into sharp relief. The bolder colors are concentrated near the center, where they will have greater impact. Most of the flowers are inserted to face up and out, rather than straight forward. This gives the arrangement a dynamic, lifted quality.

Light pink crepe myrtle, gerbera daisies, roses, and alstroemeria carry the pink of the magic lilies through the design. One cluster of crepe myrtle is recessed very deeply to provide a sense of depth at the focal point. The focus is created with a shock of color, using magenta gerbera daisies and orange zinnias. The unexpected combination of colors has a lively effect and leads the eye to perceive a connection between the flowers and the rust-colored sofa.

Thick clusters of purple statice fill in to accent the pink flowers and extend the composition toward the objects on the table. For a touch of yellow that perks up the group, the chrysanthemums and gerbera daisies are placed at the edges of the arrangement. Positioning the flower faces to look up, out, or back rather than directly forward subdues their impact so that they do not overwhelm the color scheme.

Finishing the arrangement is a matter of adding final highlights and filler and making sure the back of the design has a "bustle" to keep it from looking flat. White daisy chrysanthemums reinforce the white hydrangea and further relate the flowers to the colors in the setting. With several blossoms to a stem, they create a gently curving path that climbs up through the arrangement. Tucking one chrysanthemum at the basket's edge softens and illuminates the base of the arrangement. Foliage of gold-dust aucuba hides the underpinnings and brightens the interior of the design with a splash of muted yellow. A branch of Japanese maple inserted at the front of the arrangement brings the design forward and further loosens its base.

An arrangement with so many branches and large flowers requires a sturdy base. For this one, a ceramic bowl inside the basket holds blocks of florist's foam covered with wire mesh, which is securely taped to the bowl.

In this open sun-room, the colors and textures of autumn are drawn indoors and focused on a basket brimming with flowers. Although most of the blossoms are florist's types, the use of line material from the garden adds character and interest to the collection. The twig basket, with its handle of plaited rose branches, offers a rustic look that ties it to the deck and woods outside.

To establish the framework, maple branches, cotoneaster, and pineapple sage are inserted first. Red orange leaves and pairs of papery brown wings cling to the maple branches, giving distinctive character to the rather stiff stems. Pineapple sage offers supple stems with slender flowers that splash traces of bright red against the background.

To make sure the arrangement can be enjoyed in the round, the line material is placed to stretch and spread in all directions from the basket. The tallest lines rise at an angle that defines a dynamic asymmetry. The lowest branches reach below the rim of the basket for a more fluid outline.

Orange lilies go in next, placed at the rim of the basket to give the eye a place to rest. With four blossoms on a single stalk, they have a strong impact and must be positioned early to make the most of their importance.

Red gerbera daisies also have considerable visual weight and are recessed at the basket's edge to reinforce the lilies. A pink gerbera daisy is then added to balance the tall maple branches and carry color high in the design.

To fill out the arrangement, chrysanthemums, alstroemeria, roses, and cockscomb celosia are worked in by color, integrating the outline materials with the face flowers. The lighter-colored blossoms define the outside edges, helping separate the arrangement from the relatively dark background of trees. The deeper, stronger tones are concentrated around the center, where the brighter hues can frame and highlight them. The handle is also incorporated as an element in the design, and flowers inserted around it play up its twiggy character.

Carnations and statice are worked in last. The ruffled magenta-and-white carnations accent the color scheme, and their long stems loosen the shape. Statice helps add variety of scale with tiny dots of pale pink and serves as filler.

To finish, moss is tucked around the base of the arrangement, hiding the wire-covered florist's foam. This is mounded in a plastic liner inside the basket.

*M*uch of the appeal of arrangements inspired by Japanese flower art is their eloquent simplicity. Here the designer has created a crisp expression of the fullness of autumn, using just a handful of materials.

The antique basket suggested a design after the manner of the *moribana* form, in which flowers are arranged in a wide, shallow container. One of the placements dictated by that form is to the extreme edge of the container, creating a dynamic tension through asymmetrical balance.

In both Oriental and Western flower art, arrangements done in baskets should allow enough of the handle to show to give the impression that the basket could be picked up. This handle, fashioned from the gnarled and knotty roots of a rose tree, has such an interesting form that it has been left fully visible as an important feature of the arrangement. Originally used to carry charcoal, this Japanese basket has its own metal liner, which provides a level surface for the needlepoint holder that holds the flowers and branches.

The design begins with a long piece of cotoneaster, selected for its graceful arch. Inserted behind the handle, it extends slightly toward the rear. A shorter branch stretches in the opposite direction and forward, suggesting an opposing force pulling on the first branch. Additional cotoneaster fills in to reinforce this feeling of elastic tension.

Two dahlias are then wedged in place, angled so that their faces reach forward. To finish, three dogwood leaves reddened by cool weather are inserted to the side to counterweight the dahlias. Clematis vine hides the needlepoint holder and adds interest with its curly tendrils and bright green color.

A container that expresses a strong personality of its own becomes a vital decorative element in the arrangement. Here a wicker duck inspires a bright panache of flowers and foliage that emphasizes the energetic backward sweep of the wings.

To begin the shape, geranium leaves are pushed into the florist's foam so that they project on either side of the wings. The leaves at the front soften the edge of the container and fill the space above the duck's shoulders. The "tail" leaves are inserted so that the underside and profile show, underscoring the sense of backward thrust.

Stems of euphorbia stretch this line still further. To stress the linear quality and the intense orange color, all the leaves are snipped off.

Clusters of nandina berries embellish the framework. Bright red geraniums are then worked in to provide a sense of weight and a strong impact of color. The duck itself serves as the point from which the energy flows, and the lowest geranium is placed to underscore this. Chrysanthemums supply the final touch, accenting the framework and brightening the group.

The materials are worked in around the handle to emphasize the container's function as a basket. A plastic liner inside holds the florist's foam and water.

An arrangement of modest size takes on added importance when it is lifted in a pedestal vase. Because the vase itself is so prominent, it becomes an important decorative element that must be compatible with both the setting and the flowers. This pedestal vase, created by Rutherford Yeates, has a light, sculptural quality that suits the clean, fresh look of the den. A yellow-and-black Chinese print provides color that further links the vase and flowers to the setting.

The slender serpentine arm supporting the container dictates the flow of movement to be developed by the flowers. The design begins with a long, branching stem of elaeagnus to define the vertical line. Drooping leucothoe establishes the width and base of the arrangement and carries the winding movement across the design.

Red gerbera daisies and a single red tulip are placed next, forming an inverted triangle that leads the eye into the room. Yellow lilies, daffodils, and Fuji chrysanthemums then go in to form a broad triangle of color that leads the eye across the arrangement. Pink tulips and carnations help unify the design. Two stems of lavender delphiniums placed high in the arrangement provide depth, while white Fuji chrysanthemums highlight the broad band of bright yellow.

Finally, stems of waxflower and bare branches of kerria and Chinese tallow (popcorn) tree are added for accent.

In an arrangement like this one, it is essential that the florist's foam project well above the rim of the container; then the stems can be inserted so they will fall at the proper angles. To give the stems additional support, the florist's foam should be covered securely with wire mesh.

lowers can mark the year's passage with more eloquence than any calendar. Although seasonless varieties from the florist are used in this autumn design, it is the branches and garden roses that give it vibrance and life.

An antique blackamoor serves as the distinctive container for the brilliant display. The angle of the figure's body gives the cue for one main line, described with two branches of frost-touched oakleaf hydrangea. The third and tallest branch of hydrangea stretches toward the ceiling at a counterbalancing angle.

Long pieces of winter honeysuckle go in next. With all of the leaves snipped off, its decorative quality becomes apparent. The twiggy branches reach with jagged fingers into the space all around the arrangement, and translucent red berries clinging to the stems provide tiny points of color in the outline. Finally, a maple branch bearing a few colorful leaves is inserted at the back of the arrangement. It gives stability to the framework with its vertical thrust.

Gerbera daisies and garden roses are then worked in to form the body of the design. This is kept rather dense and in scale with the blackamoor's bowl, so the lacy, stippled effect of the winter honeysuckle branches will show to best advantage.

Red gerbera daisies are the most intensely colored flowers in the group. They mark the axis with one flower tucked in deep at the rim of the container and a second placed at the upper edge of the bouquet. Additional gerbera daisies link the body of the design with the outline material. To imply movement, these flowers are inserted so that they face up and back along the line defined by the tallest hydrangea branch.

Roses fill out the group. Placed according to color, they grade from medium tones to dark to light across the composition. As a result, the pink roses seem even more luminous because of the contrast with the red.

Three tropical proteas are then added to spice the group with unusual texture and subtle transitional color. The lowest protea reaches below the container for a graceful, spilling-over effect. The other two carry the line up toward the mirror.

Orange lilies and a gerbera daisy help complete the arrangement. As a finishing touch, peach-colored miniature carnations are added to extend the line of the bouquet still further toward the bowfront chest. A few carnations are also tucked into the composition for depth.

Working against a mirror doubles the impact of the flowers. This arrangement takes advantage of that effect to add depth and interest. A few gerbera daisies, carnations, and the topmost protea give the group a good backing. In addition, the largest rose, which

faces outward from the edge of the group, actually leads the eye into the mirror. Only in the reflection can its pale yellow center be fully appreciated.

The support for this arrangement is a small amount of florist's foam covered with wire mesh. To hold it steady under the weight of the branches, a strand of florist's wire twists around the mesh on one side, runs under the bowl, and ties to the other side.

reaches toward the table. The leafy branches are trimmed for a lighter effect; some are turned to show the underside of the foliage, which is a lighter green than the upper surface. Elaeagnus enlarges the outline with branches that arch, curl, and soar. Most of these stems are flipped to display the silvery underside.

Knotweed stretches the line still further. Its stiff branches introduce a light froth of color around the outside edges of the design. To keep the fan shape from being rigid, elaeagnus and knotweed incline forward from the top of the arrangement. Their contours continue through the design to emerge from the base, where one especially graceful piece of elaeagnus traces a scrolled line to the corner of the table. Branches of common privet go in low to enrich the shape with clusters of blue black berries. Privet berries also add texture and depth at the heart of the design. Horsetail rush and branches of American beech fill out the crown of the group.

With this framework in place, rubrum lilies are then added. The stiff stems are placed so that the exotic blooms face into the design. This moves the eye toward the focal area, where one upturned lily breaks the edge of the vase. Gerbera daisies are inserted next. To suggest movement without forming too obvious a line, the flower faces are positioned to look up, out, or down, but not directly forward. The red and magenta gerbera daisies go in low, close to the body of the design, where their strong color provides weight. Turning one red blossom in profile gives a pleasing line and underscores the sense of kinetic energy.

Chrysanthemums, roses, and carnations then fill in. The flowers are inserted at staggered heights to soften the shape. Tucking a few light-colored blossoms deep into the heart of the arrangement draws the eye into it, creating an illusion of depth. Dainty white blossoms of narcissus are clustered low near the focal area to lighten it, and heather fills in at the base, accenting the other colors.

To finish, yellow euphorbia and statice are worked in, embellishing the line and bringing the design forward. Miniature carnations enrich and highlight the focal area, offering a luminous quality that brings the other colors alive.

For a mass of flowers like this one, an urn offers the necessary depth and substance. To permit the insertion of cascading stems, the container is overfilled with florist's foam. Wire mesh taped over the foam keeps it from breaking apart under the weight of the stems.

A formal setting is made livelier and richer when it is embellished with a grand arrangement. Composed in a classic urn, this free-flowing design accents the elegance of the Italian baroque console table and gilded mirror. The mirror's crest of spreading wheat is echoed in the loose fan shape of the arrangement, whose graceful rhythms and proportions express those of the setting.

Branches from the garden give this group its strength and vitality. Florida leucothoe begins the framework, which curves high against the mirror and

One key to the success of a composition is the designer's sensitivity to the artistic possibilities of the materials. Here two types of houseplant ferns serve as a background for orchids. The bird's-nest fern, which supplies the framework, offers broad green fronds with ragged, deeply cut contours. Their irregular outline has a wild, almost primitive quality that recalls the tropical origins of many ferns and orchids.

The primary vertical frond is reinforced with a second that has been trimmed slightly to provide a sleeker, more sinuous line. A third frond breaks the edge of the vase to stretch the design down and forward. Additional trimmed and shaped ferns are supplemented with foliage of Nippon lily (*Rohdea japonica*) to define the outline's width. The foliage also introduces gracefully recurved lines that lead the eye from the vertical axis to the base of the design.

Euphorbia is positioned next. Stripped of leaves, the long stems stretch out and down, giving a sense of stability to the composition. The tiny flowers also add zest to the group with a hint of orange.

A stem of a *Dendrobium* sp. orchid then supplies a graceful knotted line to reinforce the crown. Two *Cattleya* sp. orchids positioned at the face of the arrangement give it focus, and a third balances them to the rear, drawing the eye around the group.

Light, feathery asparagus fern supplies the finishing touches. The stems are positioned to flow gracefully toward the mantel and back toward the wall, softening the appearance of the arrangement. The fern also helps hide the florist's water vials into which the flowers are inserted, and it screens the florist's foam, which projects well above the gold rim of the urn. The container is as important here as the materials and their disposition. Black marble enhances the simple dignity of the composition and offers the appropriate note of elegance.

An arrangement in green and white has the same refreshing effect as a cool breeze on a summer day. This combination of broad leaves and soft flowers set against black and white conveys the languorous mood of a mid-August reverie.

Long stems of flowers from two selections of hosta (plantain lily) establish the outline of the design. Hosta blooms progressively from the bottom of the stem to the top, a feature the designer uses to advantage. Spent blossoms were removed from the tallest stems so that the top clusters of delicate, porcelain white flowers seem suspended in air. A third stem forms a bridge between these two and the body of the design. Additional stems define the width and project toward the viewer to give the composition depth.

Hosta foliage is inserted next to strengthen the fluid line sketched by the flowers. Often hosta leaves are used as filler or undershadow in arrangements; here their broad, deeply veined surfaces are prominently displayed as the keynote of the design. Peegee hydrangea completes the solid background, above which Peace roses and rubrum lilies float. These garden flowers add soft color, but because they drift above the green near the edges of the arrangement, they do not diminish the impact of the foliage.

To help balance the visual weight of the foliage, a branch of quince is inserted below the flowers. The foliage and black berries of yellow passionflower vine provide a finishing touch, trailing from the rim of the container onto the marble tabletop.

Objects in the setting are also worked into the composition. The alabaster fish lead the eye up to the sweeping curve of the hosta flowers, while the lid of the Pontypool coffee urn is placed in line with the axis of the arrangement, where it acts as an anchor.

To protect the urn, mesh-covered florist's foam is placed in a plastic bag, which is secured to the mouth of the urn with florist's tape. Allowing most of the wet foam to project above the container makes it possible to insert stems at acute angles.

*F*resh flowers at sofa level invite guests to make themselves comfortable and enjoy both conversation and flowers at leisure. To stand up under close inspection, however, the arrangement needs to be distinctive. This one weaves flowers together in five separate containers to form a single composition, whose unusual character complements the eclectic spirit of the artist's studio.

The crescent-shaped, clear acrylic cylinders, which are graduated in height, are staggered on the black lacquer table in descending order. This dictates an arrangement with a long, low diagonal sweep that prevents the flowers from forming a visual barrier between people seated on opposite sides of the table.

Because the vases are clear and the opening in each is only one inch in diameter, no mechanics can be used. The designer must depend on the natural curves of materials to provide a fluid line that reaches below the edge of each vase. The narrow openings also mean that flowers and foliage are restricted to those with slender stems.

The composition is built from the bottom up by inserting the lowest materials first to form a matrix of stems that will hold the showier flowers in place. Hardy begonia's silvery, red-veined leaves form collars against which garden roses and daisy chrysanthemums are displayed. These are placed carefully to make sure color drifts through the composition; flower faces are positioned to look up, out, or down as necessary to move the eye along the relaxed curve of the design.

Miniature gladiolus are added next for height and line; their stiff stems, delicately wedged among the others, create counterbalancing diagonals. Euphorbia, stripped of its leaves to lengthen its vase life, accents these diagonals. Additional roses, chrysanthemums, and zinnias fill out the shape. The last material to be added is delicate maidenhair fern. Its fronds complete the curve begun by the gladiolus, and its bright green leaflets are a refreshing complement to the pinks, magentas, and oranges of the flowers. The wiry black stems also slip easily into the crowded cylinders and help soften the appearance of the other stems visible through the acrylic.

The designer whose eyes are open to nature is amply rewarded with distinctive materials with which to work. Here, branches of cork elm are used to suggest a wild, restless energy that keeps the eye moving through each arrangement and into the painting. Although ordinary florist's chrysanthemums supply the bulk and color, the addition of materials from the garden and woodlands imbues the arrangements with extraordinary vitality and character.

The painting *Winter Adirondacks*, by Paul King, is more effectively enhanced by three arrangements than it would be by the usual single composition or even a pair. Framing its muted tones with flowers and foliage of related but more intense hues suggests atmospheric perspective and strengthens the illusion of distance in the painting.

Cork elm is positioned first to establish the line linking all three. The tallest limbs frame the painting on each side. In the center arrangement, a slender branch sweeps below the mantel and continues the strong diagonal begun in the vase on the left. Additional spidery branches balance this thrust and carry the movement up across the picture frame.

The outline is then reinforced with euonymus and seedpods of hosta (plantain lily). Removing most of the leaves from the euonymus plays up the seed capsules and the sculptural quality of the branches.

Developing the three arrangements proceeds by working back and forth between the center group and the two side ones to ensure a balanced, harmonious whole. In each of the urns, the dense, green berry clusters of Nippon lily (*Rohdea japonica*) are positioned next. The stems are short and thick, so they are most easily inserted before the florist's foam becomes crowded with other stems.

The body of each side arrangement is then filled in with chrysanthemums, cockscomb celosia, and ageratum, cued to the lavender tones in the painting. Following the structure established by the branches, the flowers carry color low toward the mantel and in toward the canvas, breaking the edge of the frame to strengthen the link between flowers and art. The deepest colors are concentrated close to the body of the group to provide a sense of weight and depth, while the two shades of yellow gold that float at the perimeter give a lighter, airier quality to the composition. The lavender chrysanthemums, which pick up the hues in the painting, are placed to suggest a triangle that lifts up toward the canvas, subtly moving the eye into it. Ageratum provides soft fullness and reinforces the chrysanthemums. White Fuji chrysanthemums also bring the snowy theme of the painting into the arrangement; at the same time, they supply contrasting flower form and highlights.

The center group is developed as a low mound,

Eloquence in Greenery

The sophisticated appeal of a foliage arrangement rests on the rich interplay of textures, shapes, and tones. The effect is subtle and subdued, made richer here by the warm background of paneling and rust red wall covering.

The arrangement is built by developing a series of overlapping and intersecting triangles that ensure a balanced distribution of shapes and tones. Elaeagnus establishes the upper limits of the design's height. Using a pair of stems strengthens the apex. Turning them to show the silvery underside of the foliage lifts the eye and highlights the top of the composition.

Florida leucothoe and magnolia then define a re-curved vertical that reaches back into the corner, counterbalancing the elaeagnus. Additional branches give the width, breaking the edge of the lower picture on one side and lifting in an opposing curve on the other. Because clusters of magnolia leaves can be visually heavy, leaves are selectively pruned from the stems to lighten the effect and give a more linear quality to the design.

The variegated materials—pearl-edged euonymus and gold-dust aucuba—are then worked in at the center, providing the contrast that gives the composition focus. The most strongly variegated leaves of aucuba are chosen for the place of honor. Additional branches are tucked in low to break the edge of the vase and at the rear to draw the eye through. Euonymus supplies fullness and brings the design forward.

To finish, cryptomeria is added at the base, extending toward the table in dynamic balance with the spine of the group. The thready, needle-leaved texture loosens the shape, and the cones punctuate it with their different shape, texture, and color.

Japanese cleyera fills any remaining voids. Its dark green foliage tends to recede into the arrangement, providing a sense of depth.

Although the natural weight of each branch will affect the position in which it rests in the arrangement, a foundation of florist's foam gives the designer considerable control over its placement. The arrangement can be enjoyed for weeks if the materials are conditioned properly. This involves cutting one-inch-deep slits in the stems and immersing them in several inches of hot water for about fifteen minutes before plunging them into cool water for twenty-four hours.

An arrangement can enrich an important collection, adding a lively dimension to it. Materials gathered from woods and garden offer a bold masculine quality that complements the overmantel display of hunting trophies and reiterates its energy.

Magnolia branches begin the shape, which takes its cue from the placement of the birds. The upright limb extends to the highest bird, while the lower one breaks the edge of the mantel, linking them into a single composition.

Gold-dust aucuba and nandina are then wedged into the florist's foam to fill out the shape and balance the magnolia. These materials, chosen for the variations in color and scale that they provide, add interest to the composition and help lighten the bold masses of the magnolia leaves.

Nandina berries and shelf fungi glued to wooden florist's picks are then worked into the center of the group. The largest piece of fungus and a full cluster of berries are given the place of honor in the brass bowl. Smaller pieces of fungus are tucked inside to draw the eye into the group.

For the finishing touches, corkscrew willow is inserted to lift the design and add character with twisting, distinctive lines etched against the wall. Along with elaeagnus that cascades freely below the mantel, the branches give depth to the composition and imbue it with a natural, unrestrained quality.

Using large-limbed materials calls for a sturdy base. The massive metal bowl is filled with florist's foam that protrudes well above the rim to receive the stems. Wire mesh is taped securely over it to help hold them in place. Elevating the bowl on a bamboo stand gives the group greater impact in the lofty space of the entry and keeps it from sitting too heavily on the console table. Antique Chinese vases on carved teakwood bases flank the group to frame it, providing a finished look to the setting.

The intense, clear hues of autumn foliage are so vibrant that the urge to bring the branches indoors is irresistible. Such fiery colors demand a bold design in a prominent location that shows them to best advantage.

In this composition, leafy branches of maple, sweet gum, dogwood, and nandina supply both skeleton and flesh, sketching in the outline and splashing it with masses of vivid color. The bowed contour of the upright maple branch suggests a crescent shape opening toward the crystal birds suspended from the ceiling. The lower boughs spread below the rim of the container, forming a broad, skirted base.

Flowers then fill out the shape, carrying out the analogous scheme dictated by the foliage. Red gladiolus bridge the gap between the tallest branches and the body of the design. Orange lilies and gerbera daisies in pink, salmon, and red are worked in to give a sense of weight and focus to each of the three views that the arrangement offers. Chrysanthemums, euphorbia, and alstroemeria fill in, providing transition between the line materials and the face flowers. The group is developed so that flowers and foliage seem to radiate in all directions with a loose, casual grace. As a result, flowers that can be glimpsed through the branches give depth, drawing the eye through the composition.

To finish, miniature carnations are distributed through the design. Their flexible stems relax the shape and punctuate the framework with bright points of red. Purple statice accents and relieves the vivid palette, and galax leaves serve as filler to hide the florist's foam.

Lifting this arrangement on a clear acrylic box reinforces the airy quality of the maple and permits the development of a graceful, fluid line. The extra height also stresses the importance of the arrangement.

To support the weight of the heavy branches, the florist's foam that overfills the bowl is covered with wire mesh, which is secured with florist's tape.

Bold masses of foliage accent the architectural qualities of a room and bring them into focus. In this spare, uncluttered entry, the effect is sophisticated and restrained.

Bare branches of winged elm begin the design. A forking vertical limb stretches toward the barrel-vaulted ceiling. Additional branches are placed so that upswept curves on one side are balanced by overarching, downturned lines on the other. Short pieces project out from the base to bring the line forward. This framework is then embellished according to a point-counterpoint pattern with each downward thrust balanced by an upward one. The contours lead through the design from front to back as well as from side to side so that the composition gains both depth and movement.

Magnolia limbs and mahonia provide line and mass simultaneously. Although these materials are wedged into florist's foam to hold them at the desired angles, the natural weight of each branch will also affect its placement. The designer must work with this characteristic to achieve physical as well as visual balance. While the primary limbs present the dark, glossy upper surfaces, some of the secondary branches are inserted to show the underside of the foliage. This adds variety to the tones of green and accents the group's three-dimensional character.

Gold-dust aucuba and clusters of mahonia flowers are then tucked in deep to anchor the line material. The flecks of yellow also provide interest through contrast at the focal point. Azalea branches finish the group with fine, yellow green foliage and slender contours that lighten the shape, relieving the heaviness of the darker, bolder magnolia and mahonia leaves.

hen arranged in the manner of *ikebana*, or Japanese flower art, common garden plants become sublime, expressing a spirit of serenity at autumn's turning. The goal of *ikebana* is to arrange the materials so that they suggest the life, movement, and impulse toward growth that they had in nature. In addition, the designer must place the plants with an eye to dividing the negative space around them into a series of interesting shapes. When the composition will embrace a large amount of space, the rules of the art recommend a low bowl like the one used here as an appropriate vessel. Raising it on a carved rosewood stand enhances the elegance of the vertical line that will be developed.

To begin, a tall stem of nandina is secured to the needlepoint holder and supplemented by two shorter stems. Most of the branches are pruned from all three to accent the slender lines of the stems, the lacy canopy of the branches, and the pendulous bunches of copper berries.

Next, three yellow gold chrysanthemums are inserted at staggered heights. With their faces stretching toward an imaginary sun, the flowers create a stair-step line leading from the front of the bowl back to the nandina. Balancing them with strong springing lines are three leaves of Nippon lily (*Rohdea japonica*), grouped as they might grow in the garden.

To hide the needlepoint holder and suggest an earthy foundation, pieces of shelf fungus are tucked around the base. One ragged piece projects above the rim of the bowl for an unexpected texture that adds interest.

Foliage of Nippon lily lasts quite well in arrangements when properly conditioned. As is the case for most foliage, this involves briefly placing the cut ends in hot water to expel air bubbles that form when the stem is cut, then submerging the leaves in cool water for twenty-four hours.

ven in winter, the garden offers materials that bring a touch of life and color indoors. Nandina's clusters of bright red berries and its Oriental character inspired this Japanese-style composition arranged in an antique bronze vase. The clean simplicity of the design complements the hall chest of drawers and mirror. In addition, the sparing use of plant materials permits the luxury of indulging in *Dendrobium* sp. orchids and out-of-season spring flowers.

Each element's own rhythm of growth guides its placement in the design. This roughly follows the traditional structure of three parts representing heaven, earth, and man. A single nandina branch, carefully pruned to enhance its sculptural quality, is inserted first at a nearly vertical angle. It is given just enough twist to suggest the natural growth of the shrub.

At the base of the design, three red tulips are placed to look as if they have sprung naturally from the earth. These bright flowers provide the focus and point of origin for the gentle, undulating line of color that flows upward through the arrangement.

Sprays of orchids form the third element, balancing the tulips and nandina. The angle of their position suggests a dynamic tension that imbues the design with energy. Three stems of Dutch irises, placed to give the effect of multiple blossoms on a single stalk, fill in the outline, and a dozen narcissus soften the rim of the vase. The fragrant narcissus together with the orchids suggest a flowering hedge through which one is privileged to glimpse a private garden.

To finish, galax leaves are tucked in at the back of the design. They hide the crumpled wire mesh which is packed into the vase.

The desired effect in Japanese flower art is to capture nature's beauty in a single moment of growth, but sometimes nature must be modified to achieve this goal. In this case, the nandina did not have a cluster of berries at the top, so a cluster was wired in place to bring the note of red all the way through the arrangement. Accessories also play an important role. Here, a walnut burl base gives the whole composition a more finished look by providing a bridge between the legged vase and the chest top.

When fruit is liberated from its conventional context and treated purely as an element of design (*previous page*), its decorative possibilities can take a startling and delightful turn. Here flowers and foliage combine with sliced and whole fruit for a composition that is both satisfying as a whole and appealing in its details.

Bare, jagged branches are wedged into the florist's foam to define the fan shape. To keep the fan from being too regular in shape, the highest branch is inserted at a slight angle toward the wall.

Drooping leucothoe, variegated euonymus, and split-leaf philodendron go in next to embellish the shape. The leucothoe helps soften the rigidness of the branches, and the philodendron leaves add fullness and a dynamic, bold quality. The euonymus is inserted with foliage facing upward, providing variety among the greenery with a splash of yellow.

The cross section of watermelon is wedged into position next, secured to the florist's foam with three florist's picks. Because it is relatively large, the slice is angled and pushed back into the arrangement to keep it from being overwhelming. A second wedge of melon, also on three florist's picks, goes in high to lift and draw the eye back into the arrangement. A pair of apples that rests on the foundation is secured with florist's picks as well.

With most of the heavy materials in place, the pink gerbera daisies are then worked in methodically, starting at the rear and moving to each side and forward. The pale flowers extend to the outside edges of the arrangement, reaching well up into the space defined by the branches and extending down to the sideboard. A pair of deep pink gerbera daisies inserted toward the back gives a sense of depth and pulls the eye through the design.

Filling in the composition then proceeds with limes, pears, and apples inserted according to color and shape, creating balance and movement into and out of the composition. Wooden florist's picks hold the fruit in place. To finish, a single spray of magenta-colored orchids is inserted to reach across the melon slice. This further subdues the melon's effect. Variegated euonymus fills in, softening the edge of the bowl and supplying fullness. Finally, sheet moss is tucked around the stems and picks to cover the florist's foam.

To link the composition to the sideboard's surface, coconut halves, papayas, limes, and sliced kiwifruit are arranged at the base of the container. For a colorful, whimsical touch, strawberries strung on florist's wire are placed to trickle over the edge and into the bowl of one coconut. The other coconut half, also filled with berries, balances it on the opposite side, facing toward the rear to avoid too stiff a symmetry. Rose-colored candles supply the finishing touch to reinforce the pink color scheme.

An arrangement including cut fruit is usually at its best for only one day. If the composition is prepared the day before a party, the fruit can be covered with plastic wrap until just before guests arrive. The wonderful aromas of the cut melons and strawberries add a pleasant dimension to the enjoyment of the design.

A favorite work of art gives even more pleasure when it is enhanced with a specially designed arrangement. Here materials chosen to pick up elements in the Chinese screen are combined to create a lively interpretation of the stylized landscape.

Because branches and grasses almost necessarily embrace a large space, the design requires a wide, shallow base. An old copper cooking vessel resting on a wooden slab fills the need and suits the textures and colors of the plants. To receive the materials, a heavy needlepoint holder is placed in the center of the container and surrounded with rocks. These fill the dual role of hiding the mechanics and suggesting the ground from which the plants spring.

To begin, long stems of zebra grass are inserted, forming a geyser of foliage that serves as the backbone of the design. Branches of bittersweet go in next, etching rugged, free-flowing lines that accent the grasses and spill over the mouth of the vessel. To give weight and breadth to the base of the design, maple leaves are then inserted at the front and rear.

With foliage and woody materials in place, the flowers are then worked in. White sedum is inserted low to balance the grasses. Other stems are clipped short and pushed back into the group so that the finely textured flower heads seem to hug the rocks.

The remaining flowers accent the rhythms of the framework materials with points of color. Yellow roses and white chrysanthemums form a dramatic diagonal that sweeps through the arrangement from front to back as well as from periphery to focus. To keep the face flowers from forming a pair of "eyes," the lower chrysanthemum is recessed while the higher one is tucked among the grasses and angled to look upward. Spikes of violet blue monkshood balance this dominant line and bridge the gap between lofty, linear grasses and bittersweet and the low base. As a finishing touch, two scarlet roses and one stem of red cockscomb celosia are added. These serve as a subtle foil for the light colors while offsetting one another.

To the creative eye, nature's own art forms provide the most exciting design possibilities imaginable. Gooseneck gourds offer the point of departure here, stamping the arrangement with the kind of distinctive character that makes a display memorable.

The three gourds in the vase are fixed into the foundation first. The designer decides on the angle of placement for each, then carefully punches a small hole in its shell, using sharply pointed scissors. A hyacinth stick inserted into the hole secures the gourd to the florist's foam. The fruit is positioned so that the writhing forms push the eye through the composition and direct the flow of energy into the room. The pineapple is placed next, its foliage forming a coarse rosette that anchors the gourds visually. A pair of wooden florist's picks holds it at the desired angle.

With these heaviest elements in place, the longest pieces of greenery are then inserted to define a broad crescent. Elaeagnus stretches toward the ceiling and out across the edge of the cabinet. Additional elaeagnus and two types of holly, Burford and Pernyi holly, reinforce these lines and break the crescent to keep the shape from being rigid.

Apples, grapes, and tangerines on wooden florist's picks are worked in next. The fruit is pushed in close to the foundation, breaking the edge of the iron bowl and giving an impression of color in the body of the composition. "Mushrooms" made from dried slices of osage orange add a natural woodsy texture that complements the character of the gourds.

The framework is then filled out with holly branches, which stabilize the crescent by reaching back into the corner. Branches also bring the design forward beyond the edge of the cabinet, reinforcing the impression of depth. To finish, additional fruit, holly, and a fourth gourd are placed around the base of the stand that elevates the vase. The position of this gourd is especially important because it brings the composition's swirling movement below the base to ground it. The fruit, casually arranged to seem artless and natural, accents the arrangement with a note of color and adds a lush quality.

The gourds, which were purchased when green and allowed to dry, will last indefinitely and can be reused in other arrangements. The rind is peeled off the dried fruit to reveal a buff-colored shell.

The vase, an iron bowl in which florist's foam is mounded, becomes negligible in this arrangement, giving center stage to the gourds and their explosive frame of greenery. Shadows and highlights created by recessed lighting overhead dramatically enhance the overall effect.

Foliage arrangements are a refreshing alternative to flowers, especially in winter when the garden's offerings are limited primarily to evergreens and branches. A close look at such materials reveals a wealth of forms and textures from which to choose.

Here a few branches and less than a dozen leaves are combined into an exquisitely light, linear arrangement. A serendipitous result of arranging the foliage against the mirror is that the reflection becomes part of the design, creating an illusion of greater breadth and depth. The natural posture of each material guides its placement. Winter honeysuckle offers gracefully arching branches that trace broad curves up toward the mirror's crest and down to the dresser.

A shapely bough of Japanese andromeda is chosen to reinforce the ascending line. Its irregular branching form also counterbalances the down-swept stem of winter honeysuckle and brings the design forward. A second shorter branch projecting from the mouth of the temple jar balances the upward thrust. In addition to its line, Japanese andromeda adds delicate mass. Leaves are selectively removed where necessary to lighten the branches and accent their linear character.

Leaves of cast-iron plant are then inserted to fill the spaces carved by the branches. Their broad, dark green forms and leathery texture provide a pleasing contrast to the fine tracery of the framework.

Finally, arum lily and fatsia leaves are inserted to supply fullness, weight, and textural contrast at the base of the group. The interplay of shapes and tones gives this area a lively energy while providing mass that anchors the branches.

Foliage arrangements can last for weeks if materials are properly conditioned and the vase is kept filled with water. Because the temple jar is so deep, a glass jar that fits the opening exactly is dropped in place to hold the florist's foam.

A pair of Chinese urns filled with bittersweet demonstrates what striking results can be achieved using only fruit-laden branches. The success of these arrangements owes as much to the sensitive blending of material, containers, and setting as to the skillful disposition of the branches.

The near-perfect color link between the bittersweet and the orange figures on the *famille noire* urns gives the grouping an eye-pleasing harmony. The white wall background shows to best advantage both the color of the plant's fruit and the exquisite, searching quality of the branches.

When the fruit of this sprawling shrub ripens in early fall, the yellow covering on its berry-shaped capsule flares back to display a pair of red seeds. The showy fruit lasts for years, but spraying it with clear plastic will help keep the capsules from shriveling and dropping.

Developing this pair begins by defining the line, using the longest stems. These reach up, out to each side, and forward, extending beyond the edge of the table. The initial lines are then accented and filled in with the remaining stems, which are inserted so that all seem to emanate from a central point. Positioning some branches to reach toward the rear prevents flatness, which would diminish the spontaneous character of the arrangement.

Because the branches do not need water, the mechanics are simply chunks of dry florist's foam wedged into the mouths of the urns. The foam projects several inches above the opening to permit branches to be inserted at low angles. A grid of cellophane tape over the mound helps keep stems in place.

Arrangements for Special Occasions

Parties

lowers for a banquet must have special grandeur, and a fountain of blossoms welling from a sleek glass vase makes an unforgettable impression.

Each arrangement has a casual look, but does demand skill and patience to compose. The design must be light and airy in keeping with the glass. The stems must also be carefully balanced to support each other.

Long whips of elaeagnus begin the arrangement. The secondary branches of this shrub angle sharply backward, making them useful for holding other stems in place at the mouth of the vase. To show clean lines through the glass, the stems are stripped of leaves along the portion below water.

Horsetail rush is inserted next. The bottom of each stem is cut on a slant, in the Japanese manner, to fit against the side of the vase. This keeps it from shifting too much in the arrangement.

Common privet berries loosen the outline and supply interesting texture. Rubrum lilies are the most important flowers in the group and so are positioned next. Placing them high in the composition draws the eye to the top of the arrangement, emphasizing the impression of soaring height and lightness.

Gerbera daisies are then inserted. The flowers have thick stems which must be wedged into the small mouth of the jar early or they might not fit at all. The stems are wired to hold the large flower faces where they are wanted.

The stems inserted up to this point extend well into the vase and form part of the design, defining a strong, upward thrust. The remaining flowers are held in place by the interlocking branches already positioned. Their stems do not show through the glass, thus avoiding a cluttered appearance.

To fill out the spray, heather, chrysanthemums, roses, and carnations are then worked in. Placing the deepest colors at the base provides a sense of weight to balance the spreading crown, while drifting the paler colors at the top expresses lightness.

To finish, yellow euphorbia and statice are added, brightening the pink scheme, and miniature carnations broaden the base. One long stem of sawgrass is also slipped in. Drawing a fine soaring line below the elaeagnus, it accents the airy quality. A begonia leaf tucked in low softens the edge of the vase, hiding the tightly wedged stems and suggesting a sense of presentation.

Developing the arrangement in the round almost automatically ensures depth. The flowers that face guests on one side provide a mere hint of color and an impression of fullness when seen from the opposite side.

The ornamental value of fruit and vegetables becomes quite literal when they are sculpted in bronze and dipped in silver. Combined with real fruit and vegetables, they make a striking and witty centerpiece for a dinner party.

A silver platter serves as the base for the arrangement. In its center, a silver chafing dish stand elevates the pumpkin as the largest and most important element. A mixture of real and silver fruit and vegetables is then piled around the stand to hide it entirely. Flowering kale, apples, grapes, and a pineapple are propped against the stand to hold the desired position. The kale and grapes are allowed to spill over the edge of the platter to relax the group. Arranging the silver eggplant and additional fruit on the table itself reinforces this effect and helps draw the candlesticks into the still life.

With the arrangement as the keynote of the table, the places are set with mirrors and Green Minton china, which offer the same spirit as the sculpted vegetables and fruit.

Flowers can make a dramatic difference in an impersonal setting, enhancing even the most elegant public places or private clubs. In this dining room, flowers set against the wall are out of the way of guests, yet extravagant and prominent enough to make an impact.

The design begins with elaeagnus, knotweed, and Florida leucothoe. Elaeagnus soars toward the ceiling in a sweeping curve. The branch is turned to show the silvery underside of the foliage, playing up its shimmering quality. Lower branches cascade nearly to the floor. Additional elaeagnus and stems of Florida leucothoe then fill in, giving the outline depth by arching forward and reaching back toward the wall.

Knotweed reinforces the elaeagnus. Expressing an ebullient, unrestrained energy, it stretches upward and extends out into the room. Branches of privet berries accent the framework and add a fine, stippled texture.

Rubrum lilies are positioned next. Each stalk holds the blossoms and buds rather stiffly on long stems so that a single stalk scatters color over a considerable area. One stalk reinforces the tallest piece of elaeagnus and two others fall below the edge of the urn, bringing the design forward.

The arrangement is then built up one color at a time with carnations, roses, bunches of narcissus, and three kinds of chrysanthemums. The usual guidelines for color placement dictate that the boldest, heaviest colors be placed low in the composition. Here that concept is turned upside down. The red and deep pink flowers arch across the top of the arrangement, while the white Fuji chrysanthemums and gerbera daisies extend to the outside and lower edges. Clusters of white daisy chrysanthemums and bunches of narcissus are worked in as highlights. The result is a dramatic sense of lift that underscores the baroque exuberance of the design.

Pink, peach, and bronzy flowers fill in around the red roses and gerbera daisies for an overall impression of rose pink. Gerbera daisies and carnations are also pushed in among the stems of the red flowers to suggest depth. Yellow euphorbia and statice and orange miniature carnations accent and embellish the lines. Finally, a thick bunch of heather and a cluster of miniature carnations are tucked into the base of the design, where they soften the edge of the urn. Deeply recessing these flowers gives the arrangement a bowerlike quality.

A flamboyant arrangement like this one requires sturdy underpinnings. Florist's foam overfills the urn and is covered with wire mesh. This keeps the material from breaking apart under the weight of so many stems.

An alfresco luncheon becomes a grand occasion when a magnificent topiary of flowers presides over the table. The festive color scheme takes its cue from the seat cushions and Italian china.

Creating the floral fantasy begins with the trunk, made of corkscrew willow branches wired together at the top and bottom. A cup filled with florist's foam is wired to the top to receive the stems. Building the spray of flowers then proceeds with blossoms inserted by color, beginning with oranges and reds. Ranunculuses, gerbera daisies, and lily-flowering tulips supply these warm tones and define the boundaries of the shape. This is kept spherical at the top, but stretched longer at the bottom with stems that extend well below the foundation to suggest the graceful effect of streamers. Flowers are also tucked in close to the foundation to draw the eye into the group.

Pink tulips and freesias go in next, stretching the line still lower below the spray and breaking the uniformity of the shape at the top. The pink flowers also give the group a sense of focus and help lighten the potentially overbearing effect of the warm colors. Delphiniums then go in to balance the topmost tulip, and cornflowers are worked in all around to accent the shapes and intensify the other colors. The yellow tulips and alstroemeria are inserted last to supply a touch of sunshine in the arrangement. To finish, stems of bear grass are slipped in all around. The fine, clean lines of this material loosen the group with an extravagant fluid quality.

To hold the topiary of flowers in place, the trunk of corkscrew willow is wedged securely into a heavy pot filled with moist soil. The pot is placed in the center of a tray and surrounded by blocks of water-soaked florist's foam. This is covered with sphagnum moss and filled in with Lenten roses, pachysandra, and ivy to suggest a garden at the base of the tree.

<figure>A topiary of flowers and fruit at the entry welcomes guests with a grand and elegant gesture. Like most other flower designs, the process begins with the framework. Short sprigs of aucuba, euonymus, and the Aureo-variegata selection of elaeagnus go in first, breaking the edge of the urn and projecting beyond it to create a longer, more graceful line. Foliage also goes in at the apex to define the crown. Additional leaves and sprigs are then worked in.</figure>

Filling in with fruit and flowers begins with yellow grapefruit, pears, and miniature pumpkins (available at specialty greengrocers' shops). Secured to the foundation with wooden florist's picks, the fruit is positioned to suggest a garland looped around the tree. Gerbera daisies, tulips, and freesias are then worked in one type at a time, distributed evenly over the form. To create an impression of rich depth over the whole topiary, the flower stems are clipped to different lengths so that some blossoms rest against the foundation while others project well above it. Movement around the form is achieved by placing flowers to face upward along the ribbon of fruit. This line is filled out with grape clusters, kiwifruit halves, and pomegranates.

To finish, ranunculuses, daffodils, and chrysanthemums are worked in to cover the form, using the same layering approach as with the gerbera daisies, tulips, and freesias. Greenery is added as necessary to hide the foundation, which consists of a dowel connecting a graduated series of plywood circles. The dowel is anchored in a container which fits inside the urn. Water-soaked florist's foam is packed tightly into the plywood shelves and covered with wire mesh to hold the flower stems and fruit.

In a crowded room, one dramatic arrangement elevated above eye level will make an immediate impact, stressing the special nature of the occasion. This carved marble mantel offers a suitably elegant showcase for an elaborate display. The lavish explosion of flowers and foliage conveys an ambience of contagious celebration.

Armloads of branches and garden greenery are wedged into the foam-packed container first to frame the arrangement. The outline expresses an exuberant, vital energy unrestrained by the perimeters of the mantel. Huckleberry branches stretch the design beyond the ends of the ledge as well as forward, falling across the carved frieze of the fireplace. A gracefully curved branch marks the vertical line that extends the composition into the mirror. Sugar maple, knotweed, Florida leucothoe, elaeagnus, and Burford holly accent these lines and compose the framework. The blue black berries of common privet are also added for a fine, stippled texture.

Because the rubrum lilies are both large and special, they are inserted next, reinforcing the outline. The display is then built up color by color to create a rich mass. As stems are inserted, the flowers are positioned to look up, out, or down, keeping the eye moving around and through the design. Gerbera daisies, roses, and chrysanthemums in shades of lavender, pink, and red create an impression of flowers blooming in riotous profusion and tumbling over the mantel's edge. Carnations help carry through the pink theme. They are almost always included in such arrangements because their stems have a looser, more fluid quality than most purchased flowers, which tend to be rather stiff. White lilies, Fuji chrysanthemums, and daisy chrysanthemums provide highlights and subtly link the flowers to the mantel.

To finish, heather and yellow statice are added as filler. Slender blades of sawgrass are also worked in to arch expansively over the front of the design.

Although this arrangement requires a wealth of flowers, it avoids an overstuffed appearance by making skillful use of voids. These gaps allow the individual personalities of the flowers to show. In addition, some of the face flowers and filler material are pushed in deep among the stems and foliage, where they give hints of color. This gives an impression of great depth and draws the eye into the design.

For a massive group of flowers such as this one, the container can be utilitarian, and is overfilled with florist's foam covered with wire mesh. For extra security, it is taped to the mantel with florist's tape.

Weddings

For a small wedding, the bride may eschew all flowers except those at the altar, where a pair of arrangements on the retable stresses the sacramental nature of the ceremony.

In a church with rich, dark woods, light-colored flowers will have the best effect. A scheme of white, pale yellow, and deep yellow is crisp and simple, linking the flowers to the white altar cloth and the gold tones in the stained glass.

Composed in deep brass vases, the arrangements begin with Florida leucothoe and a few stems of elaeagnus defining a loose pyramid. To suggest dimension and depth, some of the stems of leucothoe are inserted at angles that bring the design forward and carry it back toward the reredos. This manner of insertion also permits the designer to make use of the lighter matte green on the underside of the foliage. To soften the shape, branches are also inserted at acute angles so that they fall casually below the rim of the vases, bringing the line low and forward.

White snapdragons reinforce the framework. The placement of each stem is dictated by the curve or twist at the tip, which helps lead the eye into or around the arrangement. The body of the design is then filled out with lilies, chrysanthemums, and carnations. In each group of flowers, a lily softens the edge of the vase, while carnations and chrysanthemums carry line and color below it. Although the arrangements are designed to express a quiet formality, they are enlivened with a sense of movement. This is achieved by placing the flowers to face to the side or to the rear as well as to the front. Recessing some of the blossoms into the composition among the other stems draws the eye into the group, adding another dimension to the impression of movement.

To finish, yellow statice and white euphorbia fill in gaps with flecks of color. The smaller flower size adds texture and visual interest, and the bright yellow of the statice reinforces the carnations. The leaves are pinched from the stems of the euphorbia to accent the blossoms and the linear quality of the stems.

To obtain the strong downward thrust of stems that loosens the shape of these designs, the florist's foam must project well above the mouth of the vase. A square of wire mesh taped over this material provides a sturdy foundation for the flowers.

An important element in the festive air that pervades a wedding reception is the generous use of flowers. This ebullient display beckons guests to the groom's cake and champagne. An eighteenth-century rococo epergne lifts the flowers above the table to give the arrangement a lighter, airier effect. The heaviest materials, which make up the body of the arrangement, are inserted in the center container. The delicate epergne cups contain lighter-weight materials that enlarge the base of the design and give it fullness.

Long, slender branches of elaeagnus, garden-grown forsythia, and baby's-breath spirea establish the circumference and height, stretching vigorously up and out to create a strong sense of movement. This skeleton is given solidity with Japanese andromeda. Imported forsythia, which is stiffer and more densely flowered than the garden-grown type, also embellishes the outline, along with quince, Scotch broom, and Florida leucothoe.

Tall stems of white snapdragons reinforce the radiating lines of the branch material. White spider chrysanthemums, candytuft, and lilacs are worked in next to suggest a soft halo above the body of the group and carry color below the center container. Camellias in florist's water vials go in close, with bits of false cypress to hide the glass tubes and florist's foam.

The arrangement is then filled out with delphiniums, freesias, quince, tulips, lilies, roses, and ranunculuses. The stems are positioned to give the impression of color exploding from a central point.

To finish, ranunculus stems are tucked in, and heather goes in where necessary for bulk and fullness. The large, fluffy faces of carnations are placed last and give weight and color to the body of the arrangement.

The composition is built in a foundation of florist's foam, which overfills the center vessel of the epergne and each of the cups (which are removable).

117

Wedding flowers should serve to heighten the sense of occasion. Along with grand displays, smaller arrangements that are strategically placed convey a mood of joy and celebration. Here the mantel is draped with smilax and flowers for a casual, graceful treatment that softens the neoclassical features of the fireplace.

Before the design is begun, the underpinnings are secured to the mantel with florist's tape. A rope of California-grown smilax is then draped around these flower supports so the free ends trail down the sides of the fireplace.

The arrangements or badges at each end of the mantel are designed to mirror each other without being identical. First, a forsythia branch is trimmed so that it has a more slender effect. Then it is inserted to follow the sweep of the garland. An additional short spray forms the backing and defines the vertical line.

Tulips reinforce the framework and carry it to the side. The yellow blossoms provide the strongest color in the group, so they are kept close to its body, and the white tulip stretches the line of forsythia.

A single white Dutch iris is then inserted as a companion to the long-stemmed tulip, linking it to the badge. Placing it against the smilax ensures that it will show up well, and its purple throat adds a contrasting note to complement the yellow flowers.

White spider chrysanthemums, narcissus, and a yellow carnation are then added to provide transition from the white tulip to the base of the group. To counterweight this long, low panache of flowers, one large white spider chrysanthemum and a bunch of narcissus are then tucked in. Miniature carnations stretch the design in the opposite direction to carry the line of the tulip still further.

Candytuft and baby's-breath fill out the design. White camellias are added last, positioned to draw the eye into the group. For the finishing touch, leatherleaf fern is added as backing to enhance the pale flowers.

To form the support for the badge, heavy florist's foil wraps the bottom half of a chunk of florist's foam. A small square of wire mesh is then taped over the foam, and the whole device is taped to the mantel with a pad of foil under the block to prevent moisture damage.

accomplished with a surprisingly small number of flowers. This is because the designer drifts the blossoms around the outside of the arrangement, placing only a few flowers near the center for balance and impact. This technique also reinforces the light, airy quality of the branches. Because there is a relatively small amount of florist's foam to receive the stems, the heavy ones are inserted first. White stock reaches forward and extends to the rear, giving depth and softness to the shape. Stock also marks the design's height and width. Lilies, Dutch irises, tulips, and two kinds of white chrysanthemums are then inserted to float at the perimeter of the arrangement. Following the lines established by the branches, spider chrysanthemums and lilies also stretch below the base of the design, loosening the fan shape. To balance these, Dutch irises and stock go in at the center. Buds of spider chrysanthemums link them to the taller flowers.

Yellow lilies, tulips, and pincushion chrysanthemums are then added. Although most of these cluster inside the frame defined by the white flowers, tulips and lilies also carry bright color to the edges of the design. Inserting the flowers at various levels and working them into the back to face the mirror give the composition a three-dimensional quality.

Pale yellow and miniature carnations are drifted through to provide transitional color between the white flowers and the bright yellow ones. To finish, leatherleaf fern and baby's-breath are tucked in, covering the underpinnings and giving the center of the composition solidity. A few long whips of elaeagnus are stripped of their leaves and inserted to accent the soaring lines of the primary branches.

Building the design so that no stems show through the glass is a bit of conjury achieved with a special plastic cup that fits into the mouth of the jar. The cup holds a large block of florist's foam covered with wire mesh. Filling the jar with water ensures that it will be heavy enough to support the weight of the arrangement. To anchor the buoyant composition, the vase is placed on a black marble stand.

*W*eddings call for memorable flowers, and a special display that welcomes guests to the reception sets a festive tone. This explosion of flowers bursts from the top of the vase like a Roman candle. With no stems visible through the glass, the arrangement seems suspended in air.

Using the mirror as a guide for proportions, the designer begins with branches of ornamental pear, which define a fan shape and extend forward from the base of the arrangement. Branches of elaeagnus elaborate on this shape. Most of the stems are inserted to show the glossy green upper surfaces of the leaves. One upright stem is turned to expose the silvery underside of the foliage, imparting a shimmering quality to the body of the design. Branches of forsythia go in next, painting the fan shape with bold brushstrokes of color. The branches on one side incline slightly forward to draw the eye into the arrangement. These branches also underscore the arrangement's role as one of a pair flanking the entrance to the reception.

With the woody materials in place, the flowers are then worked in. As dramatic as this display is, it is

Christmas

A Christmas tree dressed with red bows and carnations creates a festive atmosphere and warms the grand spaces of a ballroom with a personal quality. Ordinarily this room's soaring proportions would dwarf even a tall tree; but when the tree is lifted on a table flanked by the serving tables, it makes an immediate impact and becomes the focal point of the room.

Decorating the Fraser fir begins with strings of tiny white lights, which give the tree a twinkling, starry quality. A red bow with streamers is then wired in place to the top of the tree, and smaller red bows are evenly distributed, secured to the boughs with twists of florist's wire.

The peppermint and red carnations that give the tree its character are positioned next. The stems are inserted into florist's water vials singly or by twos and threes to create individual bouquets. These simply rest on the branches, with some of the bunches tucked back into the tree to draw the eye inside.

Baby's-breath, which needs no water, also rests on the branches, giving the tree a frothy, light effect. Clusters of artificial cherries fill in with rich color that enhances the flowers, and bundles of cinnamon sticks tied with gold and red ribbons add a simple, natural warmth.

The water vials will keep the carnations fresh and are hardly noticeable among the branches. Long stems that project several inches from the vials are wired to hold the flower faces at the desired angle; otherwise, the flexible stems might droop.

A simple but skillfully arranged collection of flowers and greenery refreshes and accents important objects in a way that increases the pleasure they give. For a special Christmas display, carnations and hemlock create a grotto sheltering this delicate wax Madonna. The flower colors are keyed to her gold velvet robe and the note of pink in the brocade dress. Although they are nontraditional, the colors enhance the wax figures and shine with a luminous delicacy against the paneled walls and the Royal Rouge marble.

Hemlock branches define the crown and reach forward on either side of the Madonna to embrace her. For a more subdued effect, the branches are turned to show their blue green underside. Yaupon holly embellishes the framework and accents the pale colors with its translucent red berries.

Carnations and miniature carnations then fill in the shape and bring the design forward, softening the edge of the Louis XV mantel. Using two sizes of a single type of flower is a simple technique for providing the variation in scale that good design requires. The soft, full faces are placed to look forward, up, or to the side and are inserted at staggered depths to create movement into and through the design.

Arranged in a vase hidden behind the figure, the composition takes advantage of the mirror, which doubles the impact of the materials and gives depth to the group. The low vase is overfilled with florist's foam covered with wire so that stems can be inserted at low angles. For the finishing touch, a pair of wax angels are placed on carved stands to flank the Madonna. A third angel is secured to the mirror with double-backed tape.

enerous displays (*previous page*) flanking the entrance to the reception make wedding guests feel flattered and welcomed. Here poinsettias underscore the season, which is interpreted with a traditional red-and-green theme for a formal, dignified effect.

The arrangements are developed separately but with a similar framework so that the overall result is one of unity and balance. Myrtle branches give the shape toward which to work. To avoid a hard, formal apex, two branches define the crown. Additional myrtle branches bring the line below the rim of the urn and forward. This skeleton is embellished with hemlock, Burford holly, asparagus fern, and Scotch broom. These stretch the design further forward, backward, and below the base of the urn, giving a more fluid quality to the outline.

The flowers are then worked in following the shape indicated by the framework. White lilies are positioned first. Against the dark green foliage, they have a brilliant light-giving quality, and it is important that they be distributed evenly through the design. Inserting the face flowers proceeds with the poinsettias and red carnations, which offer the strongest value of color. Pink and peppermint carnations follow, with a few tangerine ones to give freshness to the scheme.

Because these arrangements will be seen from three sides, they must have a good backing. Flowers at the sides are therefore inserted to flow back towards the mirror, rounding out the shape.

White chrysanthemums and candytuft go in to strengthen the highlighting effect of the lilies. The foliage of the candytuft also helps to hide the water vials and florist's picks that hold the poinsettias at the desired height. To finish, lemon-leaf and leatherleaf fern provide filler. Leatherleaf fern at the back keeps the underpinnings from showing in the reflection.

taircase decorations bring a festive atmosphere to the house and convey a warm welcome to guests. A garland of balsam caught up with badges of rose pink camellias and magenta carnations offers a sophisticated interpretation of the traditional Christmas look.

To begin, fresh balsam is fastened to the banister with long pipe cleaners that will not damage the handrail. Red velvet bows and streamers are then pinned to the florist's foam foundations so that greenery and flowers can be worked in around them.

Although the arrangements are built up one at a time, they work together to lead the eye up the stairs.

The arrangement on the newel-post receives the most elaborate treatment, as it is the natural focus and anchor for the display. The remaining groups are developed as neat, rounded bouquets. Woody-stemmed material is inserted first to suggest the outline for each dome. For the small badges, this is accomplished with short bits of variegated Oregon holly, balsam, and imported coniferous material. In the large bouquet, a branch of Burford holly establishes a lifted line that directs the eye upward. Variegated Oregon holly, balsam, yaupon holly, privet berries, and imported conifers fill out the shape and sweep back toward the entry.

The camellias are positioned next, accented by magenta carnations. The bouquets are then filled out with lavender freesias, red roses, red carnations, and Paperwhite narcissus. In the small groups, the flowers are tucked in close to keep the shape compact. The carnation foliage loosens the outline so that it will not appear too dense.

In the large bouquet, the roses, narcissus, and freesias carry color below the base and back toward the entry, reinforcing the framework of foliage. To finish, yellow statice and leatherleaf fern are tucked in, filling out each composition and concealing the underpinnings.

The foundation for each arrangement consists of a block of water-soaked florist's foam wrapped with two layers of heavy, dark green foil to make a waterproof container. A small piece of wire mesh is taped over the top of this block of foam, and the whole is then taped securely to the stair rail with florist's tape.

See
P 94

*E*vergreens and berries are the starting point for decking the halls in the traditional Christmas manner. The combination of a large arrangement in the stairwell and a balsam garland draping the railing increases the importance and impact of each display.

The balsam roping is already wired when purchased and is simply swagged and fastened to the wrought-iron railing with florist's wire. Bouquets of variegated Oregon holly, mistletoe, acacia (an imported gray green foliage), nandina, and Burford holly punctuate the garland. Each badge is designed individually to emphasize the ascending line of the stair rail. A low crescent marks the foot of the stairs. The eye follows the balsam swag up to the next bouquet, which is full and round. Further up, the next badge is elongated so that it sweeps upward. In each group, Burford holly's thick clusters of bright red berries give the shape its character and color. The remaining greenery is worked in around the berry-laden branches to fill out the shape. Mistletoe is added last for the highlights its clusters of waxy white berries provide.

Each badge is composed in a small block of florist's foam wrapped with two layers of heavy foil. A small square of wire mesh is taped over the top to help hold the woody stems more securely.

The greenery arrangement on the table begins with magnolia branches, which define an asymmetrical three-cornered shape. Elaeagnus, yaupon holly, and cotoneaster define the axis and stretch the line dramatically so that it soars into the stairwell, spills to each side, and reaches forward into the room. To give the design fullness and depth, branches are inserted to reach to the rear as well. Carefully pruning leaves from some of the yaupon holly and cotoneaster enhances their effect.

The group is then filled in with Burford holly, acacia, variegated Oregon holly, hemlock, and privet berries. In a greenery arrangement, visual interest depends on nuances of tone and variations in texture as well as on the colors of the berries. Subtle differences in hue are achieved here by turning branches to show the underside of the foliage: silvery elaeagnus, blue gray hemlock, the subdued greens of the hollies. Combining needle- and broad-leaved foliage supplies textural variety. Berries supply both color and texture.

This group is composed in a large brass pedestal vase to permit the long, fluid lines that give it such drama. Blocks of florist's foam provide the foundation. Wire mesh taped securely in place over the top of the foam keeps the material from crumbling under the weight of so many woody stems.

125

*I*mported flowers in bright spring colors give unexpected snap and freshness to traditional Christmas decorations. Combining these flowers with garden materials produces arrangements that express an unrestrained energy and lively growth.

The arrangements, which are developed one at a time, are designed to be complementary rather than identical. Stems of cotoneaster, variegated holly, privet berries, and bittersweet define a skeletal framework for each group. The shape is roughly that of a fan, but using different materials to define each side of the arrangement underlines its asymmetrical balance. Bittersweet and privet also break the edge of the vase to bring the line low and forward. Yaupon holly and acacia (an imported gray green foliage) reinforce the outline, along with holly branches whose leaves have been removed to play up the dense clusters of berries.

Florist's flowers are then worked in to flesh out the skeleton. Yellow lilies and purple Dutch irises carry bold color to the crown of the design. Pink roses, bright orange euphorbia, and red-and-orange tulips reinforce the framework with brushstrokes of color that stretch and spread through the composition. To establish the focus, white lilies, Fuji chrysanthemums, gerbera daisies, tulips, and liatris are gathered into a bouquet at the mouth of the vase. The flowers are worked in among the privet and holly berries. Inclining forward from the narrow neck, they create a layered effect that suggests depth.

Peach-colored miniature carnations are then worked through, providing transition from the longest-stemmed flowers to those at the face of the arrangement. To finish, heather is tucked in for fullness and whips of elaeagnus, stripped of leaves, add character with a fine, soaring line. The mouth of each Chinese vase is small, so the florist's foam must project by several inches to provide an adequate surface for all of the stems. Wire mesh is shaped over the foam and taped in place to keep the foam from breaking apart.

*P*oinsettias herald the Christmas season with a joyous fanfare that few other flowers can match. Although pink, white, and variegated ones are now available, vivid red is still the choice for traditional interiors. Against the warm glow of butternut paneling, the brilliant flowers convey a mood of festivity and celebration.

Elaeagnus and hemlock establish the framework. Branches stretch along the mantel and fall casually below it, defining a graceful line that brings the porcelain figures into the composition. A spray of hemlock lifts the eye to the painting *Path of the Moon*, by nineteenth-century American artist Paul King. Additional greenery softens the edge of the mantel and provides a foundation for the flowers.

Red carnations are added next. The longest stems go in first, reinforcing the line that reaches to each side. The fluffy blossoms also carry the color forward and below the edge of the mantel. To buttress these primary stems, shorter ones are then inserted, creating a layered effect that gives the design a sense of depth.

Within this crescent of color, poinsettias are massed for a bold display. To keep them from being so dense that they overpower the composition, the bracts are staggered in a manner that suggests an upturned crescent intersecting that of the carnations. Elaeagnus and hemlock also pierce the crimson swath, providing the poinsettias with some sense of separation.

Finally, the last carnations are recessed into the arrangement to supply fullness and balance of color. Clusters of Japanese ardisia berries are also nestled low in the arrangement against the hemlock. The berries serve as filler and give depth to the arrangement. Their contrasting size and shape also add interest to the group.

Because the container for this arrangement is entirely hidden by flowers and foliage, it does not need to be decorative. A long, narrow, watertight container suffices. It is important, however, that the mound of florist's foam project several inches above the rim. This allows stems to be inserted at the low angles necessary for a cascading line.

able arrangements for a large party must enjoy great prominence in order to heighten the sense of occasion. Unusual containers that combine the functions of candelabra and pedestal vases lift fountains of flowers above the eye level of seated guests, giving the flowers a distinguished presence.

Spruce suggests the framework. A tall supple branch gives the height and is placed just off-center to avoid creating a stiff axis. Shorter sprigs indicate the circumference. Leatherleaf fern is then inserted at the container's edge, projecting below the vase to give the design a loose, graceful shape. The ferns also screen the bowl and help hide the underpinnings inside it. The grasslike, blue green foliage of carnations is added in the body of the group to supply dimension and fullness.

White lilies go in next, reinforcing and extending the main lines. The stalks are inserted to form a broken line of white leading the eye on an ascending spiral from the lowest point to the top of the group.

The design is then completed with standard carnations and miniature ones, which offer lavish cascading effects and rich color. Here a Christmas theme of red and pink is given zest and liveliness with the unexpected addition of orange. Large candy-striped and deep red carnations go in first, strengthening the vertical lines and carrying color below the base of the arrangement for a fluid, cascading effect. Between these two extremes, intermediate flowers are placed to emanate from the heart of the group, serving as bridges to the outermost flowers. To give depth and weight to the body of the arrangement, the stems are inserted at staggered heights.

Miniature carnations in red and shocking pink then fill in and provide accents. To finish, candytuft is worked in, reinforcing the lilies.

Explosive designs such as these require underpinnings that permit stems to be firmly fixed where they are wanted, even at acute angles. Florist's foam provides this type of foundation when it is built up in the bowl to project above the rim. Wire mesh covering the foam and taped to the bowl provides additional support for the stems.

long buffet table for a large reception calls for more than the usual centerpiece flanked by candelabra. A triumvirate of arrangements answers the need, creating a display grand enough to suit the proportions of the room.

Antique Chinese balusters serve as the pedestal vases. They express a solid architectural quality that carries over into the masses of flowers, which have the same spirit of dignity.

The middle arrangement is lifted on a carved stand and given more importance in order to form a center of attention within the formal balance of the group. The three arrangements are developed as a single composition, however, to ensure unity and harmony.

Building the arrangements is facilitated by dividing the materials evenly and placing the appropriate number of stems along each side of the table in front of the intended vase. Bare branches of winged elm go in first. A tall branching limb in the center arrangement establishes the highest point of the composition, while horizontal branches extend from the flanking vases toward each end of the table.

Yaupon holly then sketches in the shape of each design with lines that reach up, out to each side, and

down below the rim of the container. These are reinforced with a variety of greenery, creating a tapestry of textures. Bunches of Scotch broom supply a fine, threadlike line. False cypress and yew offer a fernlike quality. Hemlock and myrtle fill in with fine needle- and broad-leaved sprigs respectively. The shortest pieces are tucked in around the base of the arrangement to hide the top of the baluster.

Filling in the shape then proceeds with the flowers. These are worked in by color to assure a balanced distribution and to create paths that lead the eye around and through each arrangement. White Fuji chrysanthemums and candytuft go in first to highlight the group. Peppermint and pink carnations are worked in next, followed by the most important flowers, the white lilies and rose red poinsettias. Red carnations give depth to the color scheme, while tangerine ones enliven it. To finish, miniature carnations in pink and red fill in and accent the shape.

Converting the balusters to serve as vases requires having watertight liners specially made and fixed to the top of the pedestal. The liner holds a large block of florist's foam over which wire mesh is tightly molded. To prolong the life of the poinsettias in these arrangements, the stems are singed with a candle flame, then inserted in florist's water vials.

Contemporary artwork demands arrangements of a similar spirit. Here, candles and canvas set up a severe geometry that finds expression in the clean, linear designs of greenery and berries. At the same time, ferns offer a soft contrast to the abstract work by Kasia Polles. Unlike most arrangements that flank a painting, these do not break the edge of the frame. Rather, they are set against the plain wall to show up the delicate, lacy silhouettes.

Developing the pair begins by dividing the materials evenly so that the arrangements, while not identical, will express a similar character. The tallest canes of nandina are wedged into the florist's foam first to establish the height of each arrangment. The lowest clumps of berries are inserted next to define the base. These heavy clusters are allowed to drape casually onto the mantel for a more graceful, lush effect. Additional clusters soften the bowl's edge and give the focus. Intermediate nandina canes link the crown of the design with the base. These stems are inserted so that the leaf surfaces are angled rather than facing directly forward; this creates a sense of energy, movement, and depth. The tallest canes are placed to suggest a diagonal that leads the eye up to the painting.

Asparagus plumosus (a fern) fills out the body of each design with feathery texture and extends beyond the edge of the mantel, loosening and softening the shape. For the finishing touches, coral bead vines are inserted at the base to trail down the mantel. Additional vines project from the outside edges of each group, breaking the outline with wiry, meandering lines. Coral bead, also called Carolina moon seed, grows like honeysuckle, wrapping itself around other plants. Carefully unwinding it is worth the effort because the bright red berries and wandering growth habit offer such distinctive character. Vines gathered early in the fall must have the leaves pinched off, but by Christmas the leaves will have fallen.

The arrangements are built in wide, shallow Oriental bowls raised on carved stands. The florist's foam which holds the stems in place blends quietly with the froth of the fern so that no special care is needed to hide the underpinnings.

When it comes to dressing the table for the holidays, a mirrored dining table and crystal appointments call for flowers that are light and elegant. Roses and narcissus answer with precisely the note of refinement required. The shrimp and rose pink flowers give a subtle effect consonant with the simplicity and delicacy of the crystal basket and Venetian glass angels. The two colors play off of each other, with one offering highlights and the other intensity, producing a more lively composition than would either color alone.

Juniper and bits of hemlock go into the wire mesh foundation first. The sprigs are positioned to soften the edge of the basket as well as to give the upright and intermediate lines. The blue berries that are clustered tightly along the stems also add depth and interest to the group.

Roses and narcissus are then worked in. To some extent, they must be allowed to arrange themselves, because the stems are balanced among the juniper branches rather than being fixed firmly in place. A single shrimp-colored rose defines the axis. Its sinuous stem and the foliage keep the line from being stiff. Another rose of the same color breaks the edge of the basket. The remaining roses are placed to look up and out all around, giving the design a lifted quality. Although lower leaves are pruned to avoid a great confusion of foliage in the vase, those higher on the stem are left in place to supply fullness in the body of the design.

Narcissus highlight the pink-and-rose scheme and loosen the shape. To play up the basket handle, one cluster of blooms is placed to project through it.

To finish, maidenhair fern is tucked in around the base, giving the roses a sense of presentation. The foliage also broadens the design and lightens it with delicate texture.

In glass containers, the underpinnings must be unobtrusive so that only the clean lines of the stems show. For this arrangement, wire mesh combines with a traditional technique of using needle-leaved material to hold stems in place. The mesh is crumpled in the vase and wired to the basket handle to keep the mechanics from shifting as stems are inserted. Although this foundation is difficult to work with, flowers will last longer in it than they would in florist's foam because they can absorb water better.

IN · REMEMBRANCE · OF · ME

Churches

" . . . The experience of faith and the experience of beauty are in some measure identical." Van Ogden Vogt

The play of light through stained glass windows creates an atmosphere of beauty that lifts the heart. Flowers can intensify the experience, bringing the brilliant jewel tones tumbling onto the altar and breathing life into them.

Forsythia establishes a skeleton of rugged lines on this chapel altar. The top branches are positioned to frame the cross and the figure of Jesus in the stained glass so that these become the crown and focus of the design. Angling the branches slightly forward prevents stiffness. Long branches at the base reach to the sides and beyond the edge of the altar for a fluid, unrestrained effect. Florida leucothoe reinforces the framework with arching stems that soften the angularity of the forsythia. To obtain the desired line, some of the leucothoe is turned, showing the underside of the foliage. Branches also reach toward the rear, giving the arrangement a "bustle" that keeps it from looking flat.

This skeleton is then filled with flowers. The blossoms are worked in by color to assure a balanced distribution that results in a unified look. At the same time, the colors form overlapping paths that keep the eye moving through the design. Pale yellow gerbera daisies go in first, followed by cardinal red tulips, pink camellias, lavender irises and delphiniums, and anemones in shocking red, magenta, and purple.

The camellias go in rather high to bring a sense of lift to the arrangement and to mark the focal area beneath the cross. The other stems are placed to radiate from this point, with those at the base reaching below the edge of the altar to give the group a loose, flowing quality. To reinforce the sense of movement created by the distribution of color, some flowers are inserted in profile while others incline their faces forward. This leads the eye around the group, and recessing some of the flowers and pulling others forward gives the composition depth.

To finish, bright yellow pincushion chrysanthemums and statice are worked in, forming additional paths of color that accent the darker hues and introduce a note of yellow from the windows. White candytuft adds highlight and fullness across the body of the design.

Because much of the design cascades from the high focal point, the vase must be generously overfilled with florist's foam. This provides the surface needed for inserting stems at acute angles. Wire mesh taped over the foam helps hold it together under the weight of so many stems.

Easter is the most important festival of the Christian year, so it is appropriate that the flowers with which the church is decorated express an exuberant spirit. When Easter comes late, the traditional lilies can be augmented with a variety of spring-blooming shrubs and flowers to create a suitably lavish display. To provide the necessary impact, this arrangement is held aloft on a wrought-iron standard.

Elaeagnus defines the outline, stretching upward and cascading well below the base of the arrangement. The branches are turned to show the silvery underside of the foliage, which contributes to the overall effect of white. A few stems are inserted to flow back toward the wall, softening the shape.

Drooping leucothoe strengthens the framework with bold brushstrokes of green. The densely flowering branches of Vanhouette spirea form solid, overspreading curves that define a graceful, fountainlike shape. Both materials bring the design forward as well and effectively hide the container so that the massive group seems to float unsupported.

The framework is then filled in with stalks of Easter lilies. The trumpets on each stalk are held at opposing angles, and this gives an active, energetic quality to the composition.

To finish, branches of white azalea fill in, hardening up the arrangement by intensifying the impression of white. A few stems of Lenten roses are also tucked in.

Developing such an enormous spray of flowers and foliage requires a large, sturdy foundation. The standard holds several blocks of water-soaked florist's foam covered with wire mesh. This projects well above the container so that stems can be inserted at low angles for the cascading line.

Flowers at the altar draw the eye to the cross and beautify the setting for worship. At a tiny church in Linville, North Carolina, humble flowers from field and garden are groomed into loose, airy pyramids. Offering a look in harmony with the rustic interior, the summer flowers are keyed to the liturgical color indicated by the needlepoint altar hanging.

Queen Anne's lace establishes the outline. The top of the arrangement, determined by the height of the cross, is defined with two stems. One is placed slightly lower than the other to keep the apex from being rigid. The width of each group embraces the area between the cross and the edge of the altar. Queen Anne's lace reaches toward these boundaries on either side, giving the pyramid a softer, more graceful outline. Additional stems then fill out the shape and bring the design forward over the edge of the vase.

Close-packed heads of peegee hydrangea go in next. Arching branches reiterate the spilling-over effect of the Queen Anne's lace, carrying color low toward the altar. Other stems further define and solidify the shape, but the flowers remain below the crown to keep the arrangements from appearing top-heavy.

To fill in this framework, white snapdragons, daisies, and lizard's-tails are inserted so that they seem to radiate from the center of the design. Lizard's-tails grow as slender plumes that recall dancing flames. Their unexpected form perks up the group and injects a dynamic quality.

A cluster of mountain laurel marks the focal point. The mountain laurel is inserted slightly off-center and recessed into the design to keep it from appearing as a bull's-eye.

Yellow flowers are worked in next. Goldenrod breaks the outline, while marigolds emphasize the focus with patches of deep yellow. Black-eyed Susans are placed to float above the other flowers. This gives the arrangement an airy quality and a feeling of depth. A few black-eyed Susans also soften the edge of the container and splash sunny color below the base of the arrangement.

The yellow blossoms serve as a visual bridge between the altar hanging and the stained glass window. To further link the flowers to the window, light touches of red and purple are added sparingly. These colors also bring to life the predominantly yellow-and-green scheme. Snapdragons accent the height and width of each arrangement, while bee balm and roses are tucked among the other stems for a hint of depth. As a finishing touch, sweet autumn clematis is inserted at the base of each arrangement, trailing to the altar in fluid lines starred with tiny flowers.

It is important that church arrangements make good use of negative spaces among the flowers. If the blossoms are too densely packed, the designs will appear poorly defined from the back of the church. Lifting the flowers in compotes or pedestal vases further heightens their impact, allowing the arrangements to assume flowing, graceful shapes. To create such lines, the florist's foam must be mounded high in the container so that stems can be inserted at low angles.

he simple act of decorating the altar with flowers introduces an intangible quality of warmth and life into the worship setting. Using a pair of arrangments satisfies the need for symmetry and provides a colorful frame for the cross.

Although the arrangements must share an overall similarity, allowing them to express a certain individuality gives a more natural and visually interesting effect. The unity is established here with a crescent-shaped outline of winter honeysuckle branches that embrace the cross. The tallest branches approach the top of the cross, tracing a light, airy contour against the dark background. They may not go higher, however, because the cross is of primary importance. Additional branches balance the strong thrust of the principal line and pierce the center of the crescent to keep it from being too rigid.

Flowers then give mass and weight to the shape. Pink camellias from the greenhouse give the cue for the color scheme, which is kept pale in order to show up against the dark wood. The pointed shapes of irises and delphiniums reinforce the framework and bring the line forward. Anemones are then worked into the design, leaving the center free. A single red anemone placed high in each group serves as an accent and underscores the unity of the arrangements. The lowest flower in each group is turned in profile toward the center of the altar to direct attention inward.

Camellias fill the heart of the design and soften the edge of the vase. To keep the soft mass of color from becoming too dense, the flowers are inserted at staggered depths and worked in around projecting spikes of delphiniums.

To finish the arrangements, candytuft, statice, and magnolia leaves fill out the shapes and stretch the lines toward the altar. The close-packed bunches of statice also hide the florist's foam and the florist's water vials in which the camellia stems are held.

135

Alstroemeria: Split stems, and condition in lukewarm water reaching almost to flower heads.

To help ensure that flowers have the longest life possible in an arrangement, it is essential that they be cut and conditioned properly before being positioned in the vase. Stems should be cut with a sharp knife on a slant. This exposes more cells to absorb water than does a horizontal cut. It also keeps stems from resting flat on the bottom of the vase, which would hamper water absorption. Scissors should not be used to cut flowers because they squeeze the stem, crushing the water-conducting cells.

Flowers should be cut very early in the morning before the dew has dried and conditioned for eight hours, or they may be gathered in late afternoon or early evening and conditioned overnight. In either case, it is a good idea to take a bucket of water to the garden and place the flowers in it immediately to help reduce the shock from cutting. (The water should first be allowed to stand for thirty minutes to reach air temperature.) Flowers should be never be cut in the middle of the day, because they will not recover from the stress.

Warm (not hot) water moves up the vascular tissues more quickly than does cold water, so most flowers should be conditioned in warm water that is allowed to reach room temperature. When conditioning calls for boiling-water treatment, the flowers and foliage must be protected from the steam. During conditioning, flowers should be set in a cool, dark place to further reduce stress and moisture loss. After conditioning and before arranging, recut the stems on the diagonal, removing about one inch. Stems become waterlogged as they stand in water, and a fresh cut facilitates water absorption.

Florist's flowers have already been conditioned, but it is wise to recut stem ends and recondition them for two to three hours in warm water before arranging. Remove unwanted leaves before reconditioning.

After flowers are arranged, sugar, lemon-lime soda, or commercial preservatives may be added to the vase water to help prolong life. Studies show adding aspirin is ineffective, however.

Carnation: Cut stems at an angle between the joints, and soak in warm water. Cutting the stems under water in the conditioning container may also be helpful; adding lemon-lime soda to the vase water may prolong flower life.

Anemone: Cut when in bud, and stand in warm water up to flower heads for twenty-four hours before arranging. Before inserting a stem in florist's foam, make a pencil hole in the foam to form a well of water for the stem. Anemones need a large amount of water, so keep the vase filled.

Chrysanthemum: Break or split the woody stems of perennial types, place ends in boiling water for twenty to thirty seconds, then plunge in deep water nearly to flower heads. Adding fine sugar helps in conditioning. Annual types benefit from having their stems recut under water. The container should then be filled with cool water to which sugar is added. Strip the foliage that will be below water, because it will decay rapidly.

Begonia: Split stems and place in cool water, adding salt to the water to help conditioning. To prevent curling of large leaves, spray underside with hair spray or clear plastic spray. For *Begonia rex*, dip stems in boiling water for thirty seconds, then fill the container with cool water; let stems stand several hours.

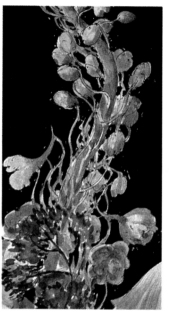

Delphinium: Cut when about half of the florets are open. Condition in deep lukewarm water, or fill hollow stems with water and plug with cotton. To encourage interesting curves in the stems, angle them in the bucket.

Dahlia: Cut as soon as flowers are fully open, and re-move leaves below the water line. Hold stem ends in boiling water for thirty seconds or singe ends with a candle flame to seal off sticky sap, then plunge in warm water. Wide stems may be filled with warm water and plugged with cotton.

Gerbera daisy: Cut when fully open but before pollen is ripe. Dip stem ends quickly in boiling water, then place in cool water up to flower heads. Recondi-tion purchased flowers.

Lenten rose: Young, newly emerged flowers will not keep well. Choose taller, older plants which are better hardened. Quickly dip stem ends in boiling water or singe them with a candle flame, then place in lukewarm water up to flower heads overnight. Make a pin hole in the stem near the flower head to allow air bubbles to escape as the stem takes up water.

Gladiolus: Cut when the next to lowest floret is ready to open. Split the stems one inch before placing them in warm (not hot) water, and let it cool as flowers stand overnight. Allowing some stems to stand at an angle in the conditioning container will encourage pleasing curves in the tips. Remove the outer green covering from buds above the highest open flower to give a greater impact of color. Adding sugar to the water helps prolong flower life.

Freesia: Flowers last well, even without conditioning. Cut when the first floret opens and place stems in cool water.

Iris: Cut when the flower emerges from sheath, and place in warm water to base of the flowers. Condition at room temperature.

*L*ily: *Lilium* sp. and hybrids should be cut when the first blooms are open, leaving as much foliage on the plant as possible. Split stems one inch or make a long slanting cut, and plunge in deep warm water to the base of the buds. Do not wet the petals. Rubrum lilies benefit from having their stems recut and split in the conditioning water. Although the flower's anthers add style to an arrangement, pollen falling

on the petals causes them to shrivel. To avoid this, remove the pollen-bearing anthers at the ends of the stamens.

There are other plants which are commonly known as lilies but actually are not true lilies; they include foxtail lily, lily-of-the-Nile, and nerine lily. Foxtail lilies and lilies-of-the-Nile benefit from adding sugar to the conditioning water. Nerine lilies need only to stand in cool water for eight hours.

*L*iatris: Place the stem ends in hot water for thirty seconds, then let them stand in cool water.

*O*rchid: Cut after the flowers have been open four to six days to allow them to attain full color. Cut on a slant with a clean sharp knife, recut under water, then stand in a vase filled with lukewarm water. Do not let the water touch the petals. Keep orchids in a cool, dark place, or cover them with plastic and store in the refrigerator until time to arrange them.

*M*arigold: Remove excess leaves, and stand stems in warm water to the base of remaining leaves.

*M*ichaelmas daisy: Cut when about half the flowers are open, and remove most of leaves. Split stem ends about one inch and dip in boiling water for twenty to thirty seconds, then stand in deep lukewarm water. Remove faded blooms. Adding sugar to the water helps prolong flower life.

*N*arcissus: Cut when stem bends to hold bud perpendicular to stem; leave as much foliage as possible on plant. Recut stems, removing one-fourth inch, and place in six to eight inches of warm water for two hours. Flowers last well in shallow water.

*P*hlox: Crush the ends of the stems with a hammer, or split them. Condition the stems in warm water.

*S*napdragon: Cut when half the flowers on the spike are open. Strip excess leaves, and place stems in hot tap water. Let the water cool to room temperature. For curving stems, stand them at an angle in the container during conditioning. Recut and recondition purchased snapdragons for at least three to four hours.

Rose: The best time to cut is at dusk. For the benefit of the plant, cut about one-fourth inch above a leaf, leaving two healthy leaves between the cut and the point where the flower stem joins the main stem. Make sure the top leaf is on the outside of the stem so that outward-branching stems will develop. Split the stems, remove the thorns and lower leaves, and place in warm water up to the flower heads.

Recondition florist's roses by cutting one-fourth inch off the stems and dipping them in hot tap water, then placing in deep cool water for at least three hours. Wilted roses may be revived by recutting and splitting the stems and placing them in warm water. Adding a preservative to the vase water will help prolong flower life.

Statice: Flowers need no special treatment. Place the stems in room-temperature water until time to arrange them.

Poinsettia: Hold stem ends in boiling water for one and one-half to three minutes or singe them with a candle flame for fifteen seconds to seal off the sticky sap. Then condition in cool water.

143

*P*eony: Cut when color shows in the bud, and remove excess leaves. Split stem ends two to three inches and dip them in boiling water or singe them with a candle flame. Then place them in warm water, and let stand for four to eight hours. Damaged or wilted outer petals may be removed to keep the flower looking fresh.

*Z*innia: Cut when in full bloom with centers tight. Remove leaves; dip stem ends quickly in boiling water. Stand in cool water.

*Q*ueen Anne's lace: Place ends in one-half inch of boiling water for twenty to thirty seconds. Stand in cool water to flower heads.

*Y*arrow: Cut when more than half of the flowers in the cluster are open. Dip stem ends quickly in boiling water, then place in cool water.

*T*ulip: Cut when the buds show color. Wrap by bunches in wet paper, and place upright in deep containers of warm water reaching almost to the flower heads. Make sure the paper extends into the water as well. Condition for three to six hours.

Contributors

Anne J. Benners

Virginia B. Bissell

Lula Rose T. Blackwell

Frances D. Blount

Mary Carolyn G. Boothby

Naneita L. Cobbs

Peggy M. Conway

Betty Jo Cowin

Paula Crockard

Mary Morén Crommelin

Betty Drennen

Beverley W. Dunn

Emmit Gaskin

Caroline M. Head

Dorothy T. Ireland

Kitty Johnston

Sue Kinnear

Charles Maloy Love

Ann Murray

Dorothy Naughton

Elberta G. Reid

Frances B. Robinson

Anne D. Sharman

Sandra S. Simpson

Anne C. Speake

Rose Steiner

Naomi N. Thomason

Carolyn D. Tynes

Arline F. Walter

William H. Whisenant

Opal W. Yeates

Elegance in Flowers
Classic Arrangements for All Seasons

Designed by
Robin McDonald Graphic Design
Birmingham, Alabama

Text composed in Linotron Palatino by
Akra Data, Inc.
Birmingham, Alabama

Color separations by
Graphic Process, Inc.
Nashville, Tennessee

Printed and bound by
W. A. Krueger Company
New Berlin, Wisconsin

Text sheets are by
Northwest Paper
Cloquet, Minnesota

Endleaves are Rainbow Endleaf by
Ecological Fibers, Inc.
Lancaster, Maine

Cover cloth is Kingston Natural Finish by
The Holliston Mills
Kingsport, Tennessee